THE HOGAN MANUAL OF HUMAN PERFORMANCE
GOLF

Jack Nicklaus once said: "I've always believed that the fundamentals of the golf swing are in a sense immutable, that all good players down through the generations have achieved certain goals demanded by the laws of physics, even though their styles of doing so or their points of emphasis may have varied."

THE HOGAN MANUAL OF HUMAN PERFORMANCE

GOLF

GERRY HOGAN

LANSDOWNE

DEDICATION

To Alexander Campbell Cook (in memoriam), the best mate I ever had. The straightest and finest human I have ever known and the most fearless. We had one hell of a communication and nothing will ever fill the hole your passing has left. You started me on this track a long time ago. Old friend, I got the job done. I "feel" your presence on the golf course and in the birds and the trees and I am a better man than I ever was for having known you.
To Professor James Lance, Neurologist.
Thank you for caring and helping me to get back on my feet when too much hurt had me about beaten. You and Professor Perkins forced me to find my own levels, my own values, and I can live in peace with what I have found. Without both of you this work would never have been done.

Distributed by Gary Allen Pty Ltd
9 Cooper St, Smithfield NSW Australia 2164

Published by Lansdowne Publishing Pty Ltd
Level 1, Argyle Centre
18 Argyle Street, The Rocks NSW Australia 2000

First published 1992 by Kevin Weldon & Associates Pty Ltd
Reprinted 1992
Reprinted 1997 by Lansdowne Publishing Pty Ltd

© Copyright text: Gerry Hogan 1992
© Copyright design: Lansdowne Publishing Pty Ltd
Designed by Warren Penney
Photography by John Knight
Cover photograph by George Seper

Models: John Senden, Fiona Burgman and Stuart McPhee
Additional photography thanks to *Golf Digest, Golf World*
and NSW Golf Association
Diagrams by Lorenzo Lucia
Anatomical drawings by Vanessa Anton

Thanks to Sanctuary Cove Resort for use of the golf course

Printed in Singapore by Kyodo Printing Co., Ltd

National Library of Australia Cataloguing-in-publication data
Hogan, Gerry.
the hogan manual of human performance, golf
ISBN 1 86302 203 1
I. golf. title II. title: Manual of human performance, golf.
796.352

CONTENTS

FOREWORD 4

INTRODUCTION 7

THE GOLF SWING — A NEW APPROACH 10

SEVEN MYTHS TO DISPEL 14

MOMENTUM GOLF 19

CONTROL OF THE GOLF SWING 22

THE SLOT 26

THE POWER OF MENTAL IMAGERY 29

BALANCE 31

THE GRIP 34

POSTURE 38

THE STANCE 42

THE BACKSWING 47

THE DROP INTO THE SLOT 55

THE DOWNSWING 58

THE FOLLOW-THROUGH 71

IN THE BUNKER 72

PUTTING — NATURAL IS BEST 74

MORE ABOUT TURNING 78

MORE ABOUT LEVERS 84

THE CONQUEST OF FEAR 89

WOMEN IN GOLF 93

POSTSCRIPT 96

FOREWORD

I first came into contact with Gerry Hogan not through golf but through cricket. It was back in 1983, about a year before I retired as a player. My team-mate Allan Border asked me to try out a new bat he'd been given, so I used it that day in the nets. I remember being astonished at how beautifully balanced the bat was, so much so that I remarked to Allan Border at the time that I thought it was one of the best balanced cricket bats I had ever used. But it was Allan's bat, and after returning it to him I heard no more about it until 1989, when I was attending a golf weekend at Kooralbyn. A tall man with a down-to-earth manner approached me, introduced himself as Gerry Hogan, and asked me if I remembered the bat, which, it turned out, he had personally designed. I told him I remembered the bat very well and asked him how he had worked out such a wonderful balance. "The same as I do with golf clubs," he replied. This was when I discovered Gerry Hogan knew a thing or two about golf.

Long before I met Gerry Hogan I had become fascinated with golf. For years I had read and analysed everything about the game I could lay my hands on. I kept filling my head with countless bits of information on technique and kept trying to put them into practice on the golf course, but somehow I seemed to be getting nowhere. As I now realize, I was actually in a state of deep confusion. During that weekend at Kooralbyn, I began talking to Gerry about golf, especially about the problems I was having with my own game. As we spoke, I came to realize that here at last was someone who really *understood* the golf swing. He told me things about golf that I had never heard before, yet they were so simple and logical I was able to grasp them immediately. Somehow, he was able to cut through the confusion and go right to the heart of the matter. For me, it was like having a straitjacket removed. Within a few months, I had lowered my handicap from nine to six.

That first encounter with Gerry Hogan impressed me all the more because I had never heard of him until then. I learned later that he was

FOREWORD

a former policeman who lived in a country town, Armidale, and did a lot of research on golf clubs in a shed at the back of his house. He had never taught golf as a professional, but over the years he had formulated a revolutionary concept of the golf swing, which he was happy to share with anyone who was interested, and by word of mouth he had gained a following among a number of keen golfers in Sydney. Further inquiries I made revealed that he had had little formal education. As a boy he had set his heart on a career in medical research, but family circumstances did not permit this, so Gerry joined the police force. He became one of the most commended policemen in New South Wales before injuries he received in the course of duty forced him to retire. Since then he had devoted himself to a lifelong passion—the study of human motion, particularly in relation to his great love, golf.

Since 1989 I have come to know Gerry Hogan well, yet my wonder at his understanding of the mechanics of human movement has continued to grow. Gerry is, above all, an original thinker. I see him as the Ben Lexcen of golf. I mean by this that he is one of those brilliant, self-taught, lateral-thinking, no-nonsense individuals that Australia seems to turn up every so often. He has a mind that knows no boundaries. He also has the courage and the faith in himself to challenge orthodox views, even when those views have universal support. This is what he does in this book.

His ability to strip the most complicated matter back to the bare essentials isn't limited to golf. I came to realize this some months after I first met him, when we had to make a two-week trip together. By now, Gerry had revolutionized my thinking about the golf swing, although, being cynical by nature, I could not help wondering if the subject was really as simple as he presented it. This is why I was curious to find out Gerry's thoughts on cricket, a sport I felt I knew a good deal about. During the trip, I often spoke to Gerry about cricket. We talked about the mechanics of batting and bowling, especially in terms of balance, which Gerry considers a key factor in all sports. During those two weeks I gained from Gerry Hogan a deeper *understanding* of cricket, of why cricketers do what they do, than I ever had during my thirty years as a player. I am quite certain that if I had met Gerry Hogan twenty years earlier and had those same conversations with him then, I would have been a better cricketer than I was.

As you begin this book, you are embarking on a journey of

FOREWORD

discovery that I have already made. You are sure to find, as I did, that it is an exciting and enlightening experience. No matter how many books about golf you may already have read, what you will read in the following pages will be new to you, because nobody has ever put it down on paper before. By the time you arrive at the last chapter, you will see the golf swing in a way you have never seen it before. You will have emptied your brain of many useless theories about golf that you have collected over the years. In their place will be simple, logical rules of technique based on the laws of physics. Not only will you know *what* to do with the club, you will understand *why* you are doing it. Unless I am mistaken, you will also be a better golfer.

GREG CHAPPELL

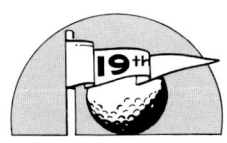

INTRODUCTION

For as long as golf has been played, golfers have been searching for the perfect swing. So far, no one has managed to find it, and no one ever will, for the truth is that there is no such thing as the perfect golf swing. There have been as many great swings as there have been great golfers, and there have been as many good (and bad) swings as there have been good (and bad) golfers. Each of us is physically unique. No other golfer in the world has your combination of height, weight, shape and strength, so no other golfer in the world can have the same golf swing. The goal of the golfer should not be to find the perfect swing. It should be to find a swing that is mechanically correct and that suits him personally.

Most great golfers have had highly individual golf swings. Jack Nicklaus's swing is radically different from Ben Hogan's, for instance, and Lee Trevino's is not like either. But if you analyse the golf swings of champions like these, you find that there is something common to all of them—there is a core of technique in each that is the same. It stands to reason that if you could isolate this "core", you would have the secret of a successful golf swing. This is precisely what this book does. **It identifies the essence of a successful golf swing, and it explains in terms of simple mechanics why it is the essence.** By comparison, some other time-honoured fundamentals of technique, such as how you should grip the club, where you place your feet and so on, are treated in this book as peripheral and are given only scant attention, which is really all they deserve.

Jack Nicklaus once made a profound statement about golf while speaking about the great Bobby Jones. He said, "I've always believed that the fundamentals of the golf swing are in a sense immutable, that all good players down through the generations have achieved certain goals demanded by the laws of physics, even though their styles of doing so or their points of emphasis may have varied." The point Nicklaus was making was that the answer to all the questions about the golf swing can

INTRODUCTION

be found only within the laws of physics. He was absolutely correct. The laws of physics determine everything that happens, good or bad, when you go to hit a golf ball, yet until now these laws have been largely, if not totally, ignored.

The laws of physics must be the very basis of good technique. The great players may have different swings, but the reason each of them is great is that in his own way he has satisfied certain basic laws of motion.

These laws are the true fundamentals of golf. The technique advocated in this book is the product of research I began thirty years ago. It is grounded in the simple but generally overlooked fact that the human body in motion is a mechanical apparatus. The body is essentially a system of levers whose movements are subject to all the ordinary laws of physics, and the golf swing is no exception. Whether golfer A hits further or straighter than golfer B is determined ultimately by laws of physics. After all, the human body has evolved over many millions of years to function within the laws of physics, and the golf swing, a relatively recent creation, must function within these same laws, too.

There is one thing I must impress upon you at the outset: **beware of symmetrics in golf!** The human brain has many peculiarities, and one of them has caused golfers endless problems. I refer to the instinctive attraction we all feel for geometric shapes that are symmetrical. We like things to be squared off, levelled off, evenly spaced or parallel with each other. If we see a picture at an angle on the wall, most of us feel an urge to get up and straighten it. As an experiment, put a picture at an angle and watch people's reactions to it. Most will be uncomfortable: some won't even be able to sit straight while they have the picture in view.

This natural craving for symmetry has had an important (and unfortunate) bearing on the way people have played golf. The inclination has always been to position the club in such a way that the movement looked to be as symmetrical as possible. The more symmetrical it looked, the more it was likely to be accepted as orthodox technique. So we are told that the club should be parallel with both the ground and the toe line at the top of the swing; that the left hand has to be at right angles both to the clubface and to the toe line at the top of the swing; that the shoulders at the top of the swing have to be at right angles to the toe line; and so on. But not one of these rules of technique has an iota of logic to support it. The theorists who set these rules were responding to a need that has everything to do with aesthetics and nothing to do with golf.

INTRODUCTION

Much of what you are about to read in this book has never appeared in a golf book until now. I will ask you to view the golf swing in a way you have never viewed it before, and many of the concepts I will present to you will sound unfamiliar. But don't be put off by this. You will read nothing in the pages that follow that cannot be grasped quite simply, for the laws of physics that determine how well you hit a golf ball are actually very simple ones. As I said before, there is no such thing as a perfect golf swing. **The golf swing you must strive to develop is the one that is easiest to repeat, that causes you a minimum of stress, and that produces the same result in ball flight every time.**

You will have noticed already in these opening pages that when I refer to golfers generally I do so as if they were both male and right-handed. Thus, the golfer is always "he" or "him", and he always has his left hand at the top of the shaft and his right hand beneath. I trust that the many women golfers and left-handed golfers (and even left-handed women golfers) who read this book will understand that I use this terminology purely for the sake of simplicity. Everything I have to say in this book applies equally to them. Indeed, because women are generally smaller and not so strong as men, it is all the more important for them to swing the club with maximum mechanical efficiency. This is what this book is all about.

THE GOLF SWING
A NEW APPROACH

A s every golfer knows, getting your handicap down is an exercise fraught with disappointment. Yet I can say with honesty that I have not known one golfer whose game didn't improve markedly as soon as he *understood* the mechanics of the golf swing. Once you grasp the fact that the body in motion is a mechanical apparatus and that the golf swing is merely another movement of that apparatus, all your ideas about golf will be transformed and you will play better golf. I do not put a figure on it. I never tell a golfer that he will lower his handicap by such and such a number. But I do promise that he will be able to play at a standard that will satisfy him. I say, "You will end up with a game you'll be happy to take onto any golf course." Not one has failed to do so.

WHAT DO I SUGGEST THAT IS DIFFERENT?

To begin with, I will invite you to consider the golf swing as a purely mechanical action. I will demonstrate that there are **two basic principles** of physics governing the golf swing, both of which have been largely ignored until now by golfing theorists. Both are simple and easily understood, so don't worry if at first they sound rather technical. **The first is the need to have all the forces of the swing working in the same plane**—or in "the slot", as Ben Hogan called it. If you master the art of dropping into the slot, you will be able to hit the ball with a great deal more power. **The second is the principle of angular momentum.** This may sound a mouthful, but it is actually the principle by which we do most things in sport successfully—kicking a football, throwing the javelin, hitting a tennis ball, even throwing the discus. In a later chapter I will describe the principle in detail, but for the time being recognize it as being of absolutely vital importance, for it is the principle by which you get the clubhead to strike the ball with maximum velocity.

This, then, is the essential theory. How do you put it into practice? First, you must forget nearly all the rules of technique you have previously learned. Most of them, believe me, are either useless or positively harmful. Nearly all are based on the widely held belief that you can consciously control the many and varied things that your shoulders, arms, hands, head, wrists and hips are doing in the golf swing. Recently, I sat down and made a list of all the points of technique a golfer is supposed to keep in mind when he swings a club. It came to twenty-seven. This is nonsense. No golfer can think of twenty-seven things in the fraction of a second it takes to swing a club. Most golfers are unable to think of more than one.

At first, this might seem to make the golfer's task hopeless. But it isn't. As I will demonstrate, **it is possible to control the entire golf swing by controlling just a couple of key movements—specifically, of your hands and your head.** All the other parts of the golf swing will fall into place quite naturally, without your even thinking about them. This is immensely important, because by making your brain concentrate on only one or two things, you will not be asking it to do more than it is capable of doing.

WHAT ABOUT ALL THE OTHER THEORIES?

There are as many theories on golf as there have been successful golfers, although you can hardly blame the teachers for this. Until now they have not had any access to information about the mechanics of the golf swing, because the subject hasn't been understood. The pro who gave you your last lesson probably learned the basics of the game from another pro perhaps twenty years ago, and this other pro may have read what Ben Hogan, Sam Snead and Tommy Armour had to say about technique and, in the process, picked up a few theories from each of them. He may have liked the way Hogan used his left arm, but he didn't like the way he placed his right foot, so he took Nicklaus's advice on that, and he preferred the way Lee Trevino took the club outside, and so on. The result is an awful mishmash of half-baked theories, which get handed on from one golfing generation to another.

Pros and amateurs have this one thing in common: they are all trying to discover the secret of the perfect golf swing, and usually they are trying to discover it from each other. The result is mutual confusion on a vast scale. A player confused about his game is easy enough to identify. You see him paralysed with indecision as he prepares to hit the ball. He stands there immobile, club behind the ball, while his brain whirrs frantically, trying to pre-pattern the swing he is about to make.

THE GOLF SWING

Nothing happens, because he can't make up his mind what to do. He's trying to remember how he hit the ball last week, or how he saw Nick Faldo on television hitting it last month, or how he pictured himself hitting it while lying in bed the night before. His problem is that he's trying to do things that are physically incompatible. He wants to keep his elbow there and turn his hands here, but his subconscious brain knows that anatomically this simply isn't possible. After an anguished pause, he launches himself into the swing, although by then he hasn't the slightest idea what he's trying to do. You can imagine the result.

THE ESSENCE OF THE GOLF SWING

I said before that the human body is a mechanical apparatus. Specifically, it is a system of levers, and to understand the golf swing you must recognize it for what it really is—a lever action. It is actually a two-lever action, because the club itself acts as an extra lever, swinging on the free hinge of the wrists. When you swing a golf club, you are performing an action that is identical in principle to swinging a flail or nunchaku, for both of these are classic lever actions. We are all familiar with the way force or speed at one end of a lever is magnified at the other. We use a lever when we prise off a bottle top with a bottle opener, and we use a lever when we sweep the floor with a broom. The wheel is a lever system, too, and one that has a lot in common with the golf swing. Consider a spoke of a wagon wheel. The outside end of the spoke (at the rim of the wheel) is obviously travelling much faster than the end of the spoke at

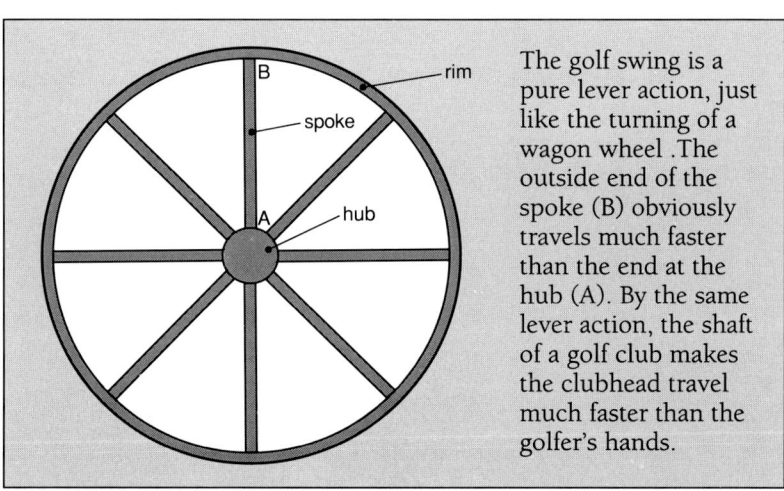

The golf swing is a pure lever action, just like the turning of a wagon wheel. The outside end of the spoke (B) obviously travels much faster than the end at the hub (A). By the same lever action, the shaft of a golf club makes the clubhead travel much faster than the golfer's hands.

the hub. Now, the shaft of a golf club performs the same function as the spoke of the wagon wheel. By lever action, it makes the clubhead travel much faster than the golfer's hands. Mechanically, this is the essence of the golf swing.

The human brain and body make up an extremely complex mechanism which has evolved over millions of years primarily to enable our species to survive. Unfortunately, the movements we need to make in playing golf were not encoded in the original blueprint of our design. We will see in later chapters that the genetically programmed movements of the human body are, in fact, quite the opposite of the movements the golfer needs to make when he swings a club. **Since we cannot change the body's design, we have to learn to adapt the human mechanism to the task we want it to perform on the golf course.** Put another way, we have to make a new and learned skill override a natural action. That is the real challenge of golf.

SEVEN MYTHS TO DISPEL

You are confused about your game and you would like to improve it. Here, then, is the first step to take. Clear your mind of the many false ideas about the golf swing you have previously held to be true. **The break with your golfing past must be a clean one.**

Most coaching books over the years have been written by successful golfers who based their advice on what they *felt* they were doing when they swung a club. This "feel" can fool you, because, apart from anything else, it takes time for nerve impulses to reach the brain. If you accidentally put your finger on the hot plate of a stove, it would be nearly two-tenths of a second before your brain received a message from the finger that something painful was occurring. As it happens, this is about the same time it takes a golfer to complete the downswing. Once the downswing has begun, there is simply no way you can tell what your hands are doing or even where they are at any moment during those two-tenths of a second. You may "feel" your hands are in a certain position, but they will actually be somewhere else, because by the time the feel has been registered in your brain the ball will already be in flight.

I would need a separate book to catalogue all the myths that golfers have been fed over the years and that most have been happy to swallow. These are seven of the most common.

MYTH No. 1
Keep your left arm rigidly straight at all times.

Most great golfers have been advocates of this, but if you look closely at photographs of them in action, you will see that few practised what they preached. Peter Thomson had his left arm bent almost at right angles at the top of the swing. Ben Hogan wrote that the arms should move together as if they were bonded to each other with giant rubber bands. In fact, there are photographs that show Hogan with elbows pointing each way and both arms bent. These two golfers, it is worth noting, won a total of thirteen majors between them.

There is nothing *intrinsically* correct in having a straight left arm, and there is certainly no reason at all for keeping your left arm straight in the upswing and in the top half of the downswing. **A golfer who swings the club correctly will certainly have a straight left arm in the bottom half of the downswing, but this is purely a consequence of doing other things in the swing correctly. It is the product, not the cause, of a good golf swing**

MYTH No. 2
Use leg power.

Your legs do have a function in the golf swing: they are for standing on. Your legs merely react to what you intend to do with your body, which in turn reacts to what you intend to do with your arms. Yet the idea of leg power is taught as an article of faith by perhaps a third of the world's golf instructors. You hear them speaking admiringly of such-and-such a golfer who can "drive the club through the ball with his legs". The idea is that the legs somehow generate the power of the golf swing. It would be an appealing concept if it were not complete fantasy. **The legs do not *generate* any real power in the golf swing at all. If they did, it would confound all the laws of physics.**

As every engineer knows, if you pass energy along a transmission chain, you will lose some of it at every coupling or joint. Now, in purely mechanical terms, the joints of the human body are extremely inefficient at transmitting energy. As a result, as much as 90 per cent of any energy you generate by a movement of the legs or hips would be lost by the time it reached the golf club. Somebody once calculated that about 4.5 horsepower has to be generated at the clubhead in the course of an ordinary golf stroke. So, if this were to come from the legs and hips, the legs and hips would need to generate more than 50 horsepower to begin with, given the heavy loss in transmission. The idea is ludicrous. Only the legs of a superman would be capable of such a feat.

MYTH No. 3
Keep your head still.

Belief in this well-known maxim goes back at least as far as Harry Vardon, who used to say that when he swung the club he felt as if he had a rigid rod running from the top of his head, down through his spine, to the ground, around which the rest of his body revolved. Until fairly recent times, golfers were taught that they had to keep their head perfectly still throughout the golf swing, and I estimate that 90 per cent of them still try to do it. How often, after you have played a bad shot, have you heard one of your playing companions say "You lifted your head"? Lately, however, more and more golf instructors have come to accept that it does no harm to let the head turn a little.

But I go further and say that you *should* turn your head to the right as you raise the club. If you don't, you won't be able to turn your shoulders as far as you need to. Furthermore, your automatic balancing mechanism dictates that as you raise the club either your hips or your head will move towards your right side, and it is far better for your head to move than your hips. **There has never been a good golfer who kept his head still. Moving your head towards the right allows you to turn your shoulders and arms in a natural, fluent movement.**

MYTH No. 4
Golf is a top-handed game.

Golfers around the world believe this to be true. How often have you heard it said that golf is a left-sided game for right-sided players? Or that "the left arm does the work and the right arm merely goes along for the ride"? I have even heard golf theorists discuss the golf swing in terms of how efficiently the left arm can drag the dead weight of the right arm along behind it! None of this is true. The left arm certainly does not control the club. How could it, when the left side of the brain, which controls the right side of the body, is more than 80 per cent dominant in the average right-hander?

Golf *feels* like a top-handed game, because it is largely a left-sided action. In fact, it is the right hand that plays the dominant role in controlling the golf swing, even if its role is less conspicuous. **It is sometimes said that the left arm produces most of the power of the stroke. This is not true, either. Neither arm produces the power. It is the turning of the torso that produces the power; the arms are merely levers which apply that power to the ball, and both of them contribute to this function.**

MYTH No. 5
The right foot must be at right angles to the toe line.

This idea is a product of the obsession we all have with symmetrics. As

Knowing what suits your body is more important for your golf swing than sticking to any of the myths and rules you have been taught. For example, consider champion Nick Faldo. A tall man, he stands close to the ball he is about to hit. By contrast, a shorter golfer like Lee Trevino, shown overleaf, gives himself more distance from the ball. The two men have different golf swings, but each is known as a master.

Lee Trevino addresses the ball from a further position than either Nick Faldo (overleaf) or Jack Nicklaus (see the frontispiece), both of whom are taller men.

I explained in the opening chapter of this book, symmetrics have provided a basis for countless wrong and often senseless rules of technique. **There is no reason why you should keep your right foot at right angles, so don't feel obliged to do it. Just place your right foot in whichever position feels most comfortable.**

MYTH No. 6
Keep the right arm pressed firmly against the side in the backswing.

Many textbooks have advised golfers to do this, the idea being that it will help them maintain the position in the downswing. To reinforce the point, they have urged golfers to put a handkerchief under their right arm and make sure it is held firmly there when they take the club back. Here is a little experiment that shows how ridiculous this is. Imagine that the back of your neck is itchy just below and behind your right ear and proceed to scratch it with your right thumbnail. As you do so, look at the position of your right elbow. If you want your right hand to be roughly in this scratching position at the top of your backswing, this is where your elbow must be, too. Now, put a handkerchief under your arm and try to scratch your neck in the same way. At once you will see how incompatible the position is with the movement you are trying to perform.

MYTH No. 7
There should be a controlled release of the hands.

The idea is that the golfer starts the downswing with his wrists cocked back and that just before impact he deliberately uncocks them, thereby producing an acceleration of the clubhead at the last moment. This strongly advocated manoeuvre (which no golfer has ever been able to perform) is often called "hitting with the hands". Now, an essential thing to know about the hands in golf is that, contrary to everything you've been taught over the years, the hands cannot generate any power in the golf swing. The hands *control* the golf swing, but they cannot accelerate the clubhead. At impact, the hands move about the wrists, which act as a free hinge.

So why do the textbooks tell us that we should hit with the hands when this is patently impossible? The reason is that when a top golfer hits the ball, he *feels* he is hitting with his hands. In fact, the wrists of a good golfer do uncock before impact, producing the late acceleration of the clubhead, but the golfer doesn't do the uncocking. What actually happens is that the wrists act as a free hinge and the centrifugal force of the clubhead combined with the momentum of the right arm forces the wrists forward. This is the "late hit" that the top golfers talk about and that all of them try to achieve.

The mere concept of hitting with the hands is harmful for another reason—it induces the golfer to try to move his hands faster. This is exactly what the golfer shouldn't be doing. By trying to move your hands faster, you will automatically retard the turning of your upper body, which is what really generates the power of the swing. It is essential to realize that you cannot consciously generate any power in the golf swing—all you can do is control the power you have stored during the backswing and release it at the right time. What the golfer ought to be doing is trying to slow the butt of the club, because this is how you achieve maximum acceleration of the clubhead. I will explain the mechanics of this in detail later, but in the meantime I refer you to the illustration of a runner hitting a trip-wire on page 20. The two things may not seem at first to have anything in common, but the mechanical principle behind both of them is the same.

So, you must rid yourself of the idea that you can accelerate the clubhead at the last moment with your hands. About 70 per cent of popular theories on the golf swing are based on this idea, so when you get rid of it, you will be getting rid of these theories, too.

MOMENTUM GOLF

Your body is essentially a lever system. If you pick up a golf club, you merely add one more lever to the system. If this expanded lever system—body plus club—is to operate successfully, it must function as a single, harmonious unit in compliance with the laws of physics. In the golf swing, the underlying principle is the principle of angular momentum.

I know this sounds rather technical, but bear with me for a moment, because the concept is an important one to grasp. Angular momentum means the momentum an object gains as it *accelerates* through an arc. In the golf swing, the angular momentum you generate with your upper torso at the start of the swing is transferred through the shoulders, arms and club shaft to momentum at the clubhead. **Contrary to what most golfers believe, you cannot generate power in the downswing.** The downswing merely releases and transmits the power that was stored when you turned your torso in the backswing. Technically, the secret of the golf swing is to lose as little as possible of this power in the transfer from torso to clubhead, which is why I speak of the *conservation* of angular momentum. The way you lose momentum in the transfer is by allowing slack to enter the system, and slack is the enemy of angular momentum.

Angular momentum is a key factor in all kinds of human movements—swinging a tennis racquet, casting a fishing line, kicking a football, cracking a bullwhip. In each of these examples we have an object—the head of the racquet, the tip of the bullwhip or whatever it may be—accelerating at the end of a moving radius. The object is thus said to be acted on by a radial accelerator. The cracking of a bullwhip is probably the most striking example of this. The handle of the whip is flicked, and the radial accelerator begins to work on the lash, curling it over and over at an ever-increasing velocity until, by the time the radial accelerator has reached the end of the lash, the tip is moving fast enough to break the sound barrier, which is what produces the crack of the whip.

The same radial accelerator works on the golfer's arms and club. It is what enables a good golfer to generate tremendous speed in the clubhead at the moment of contact and so hit the ball almost out of sight.

Here is another example of radial acceleration you may find helpful. Imagine someone running flat out across a field at 30 kilometres (20 miles) an hour. He comes to a trip-wire without seeing it, trips over it and slams his head into the ground. He was running at 30 kilometres (20 miles) an hour; but his head may well hit the ground at 60 kilometres (40 miles) an hour, because it has accelerated around a radius, which in this case is the length of his body. You can equate this very simply with what happens in the golf swing. The runner's feet, as they move along at 30 kilometres (20 miles) an hour, represent the hands swinging the club, while his head, as it whips around, represents the clubhead just before impact.

As you may remember from your physics classes at school, momentum is defined as the mass of an object multiplied by its speed. At the start of the downswing you have a large mass, your torso, moving at a low speed. At the end of the downswing you have a small mass, the

If a runner travelling at 30 kilometres (20 miles) an hour suddenly trips over an unseen wire, his head may well hit the ground at twice that speed, because it has accelerated around a radius, which in this case is the length of his body. The same radial acceleration is at work in the golf swing. The runner's feet represent the golfer's hands swinging the club, while his head, as it whips around, represents the clubhead just before impact.

MOMENTUM GOLF

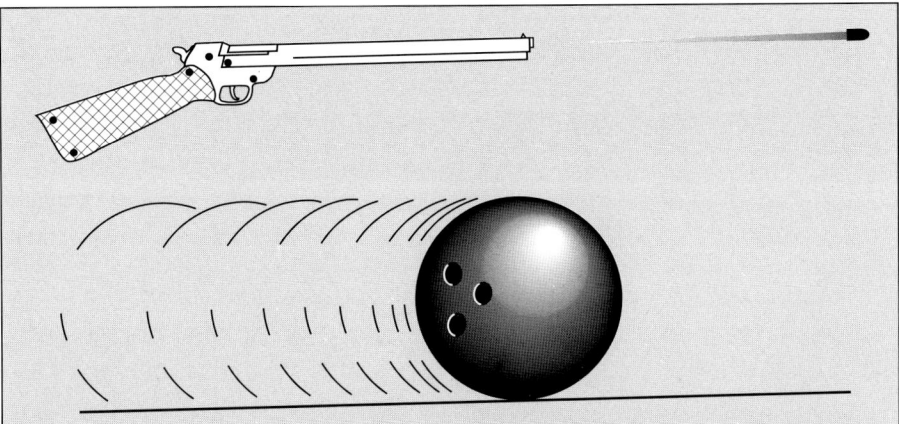

Momentum is defined as the mass of an object multiplied by its speed. A bowling ball rolling along at 5 metres (16 feet) a second has roughly the same momentum as a rifle bullet travelling 140 times as fast—the reason being that the ball is 140 times heavier than the bullet. It is the same in the golf swing. At the start of the downswing you have a large mass, your torso, moving at a low speed. At the end of the downswing you have a small mass, the clubhead, moving at a high speed.

clubhead, moving at a high speed. If you had 100 units of momentum at the start of the downswing, 95 of them might be generated by the mass of the torso and only 5 by the speed at which it turns. If you had 100 units of momentum at the end of the downswing, only 5 might be generated by the mass of the clubhead and 95 by its speed. Obviously, your objective must be to finish the downswing with as many as possible of the 100 units of momentum you had at the start.

This is where the radial accelerator comes in. Good golfers try to achieve what they call a "drag" in their downswing. This means rotating during the downswing in such a way that, to begin with, the clubhead drags behind. So their hips begin to turn first, followed by their shoulders, then their arms, then the butt of the club and finally, a long way behind, the clubhead. This forces the clubhead to accelerate rapidly just before impact to catch up with everything else at the bottom of the downswing, thus achieving maximum velocity when the ball is hit.

Mechanically, momentum is the essence of the golf swing, which is why I have sometimes described my approach to the game as "momentum golf". The term itself is useful. It helps people to think of golf in terms of its basics—in terms of the laws of physics that determine everything you can and can't do with a golf club.

CONTROL OF THE
GOLF SWING

Some time ago I was amused to see a Sydney newspaper which had been running a series of golf tips by Billy Casper publish golf tip number 500. Imagine that—500 things for the golfer to worry about in the nine-tenths of a second he takes to bring the club back and swing it down! On that same day I happened to be listening to a cricket broadcast and heard one of the commentators draw Fred Trueman's attention to the same item. "Fred, what do you think of Casper's 500th tip?" he asked. "It could prove very useful," Trueman replied, "provided I hadn't forgotten the other 499." He obviously saw the absurdity of it.

Nine-tenths of a second! What can do a golfer do in such a fleeting moment, given the time it takes for muscles to contract, nerves to carry impulses and the brain to process information? In considering this question, it is essential to recognize that any movement you make, however complicated, has to be pre-programmed by the brain. In other words, the brain organizes the movement in advance. For the golfer, this means that you cannot possibly begin your downswing according to one advance programming and then, halfway through the swing, switch to another. It is physically impossible for anyone to perform more than one or two consciously controlled movements in two-tenths of a second, the duration of the downswing. The body's muscles and nerves simply don't allow it.

Let us apply this to the golfer. When he swings a club, he is performing one visible action, but it is one that consists of many separate movements performed in sequence. We have already seen how most golfers are incapable of consciously controlling more than one movement in the downswing. All the other movements in the downswing must somehow fall into line with the one you control, which I will call the prime mover. This is true of even the simplest actions we perform. Take the act of walking. There can hardly be anything more straightforward than this. Yet if you had to think consciously of all the things your body does when you walk—where your feet are, how far you are swinging your arms, what muscles need to be pulled to keep yourself balanced, whether one leg is in sequence with the other—you wouldn't be able to go two paces. In golf, the secret is to have your brain program a golf swing that has the right prime mover. If you accomplish this, you will play better than you could have imagined. **If you try to consciously control more than one element of your swing, you are sure to make a mess of it.**

Look around you on any golf course at the weekend and you will see what I mean. It is the single most common mistake that weekend golfers make—trying to control all the various moving parts of their bodies when it is physically impossible for them to do so. So you see them trying to manoeuvre their legs, hips, shoulders, arms, all at the one time. What they're really doing is trying to control involuntary actions over which they have no control. You'll see a golfer trying to shift his hips in a certain direction. But because of the way he is swinging his arms his brain wants his hips shifted in a different direction. The result is anatomical confusion.

The key to the golf swing—and here I am getting close to the very essence of the art of playing golf—is to leave alone the things you can't control so that you can concentrate better on the one thing you can control. Then you will have an efficient reaction chain which will repeat itself endlessly, provided you leave its component parts alone. Now, it is obvious that each link of a reaction chain depends on the link that precedes it. If you get link A right, Z will be right, too. But if A is only 90 per cent right, Z will probably end up being only 20 per cent right, because the whole chain will be different.

There are two centres of control in the golf swing—your hands and your head. The hands are the dominant part of the body. What you intend to do with them invariably dictates how the rest of the body moves. The hands can't move themselves, of course. They are completely dependent on the arms for every movement they make. Yet the arms are the slaves of the hands. The reason the arms move is nearly always to position the hands. In other words, what you intend to do with the hands dictates where and how the arms move. It is this physical characteristic that we make use of in the golf swing. The hands cannot power the golf swing, but they do control two of the primary levers in the swing— namely, the arms—so, effectively, they control the swing.

Let us now examine how the hands manage to exercise the control, for this is an absolutely key element in the golf swing. It all gets back to what the hands are fashioned by nature to do. Basically, the hands are designed to take food to the mouth, which means they are genetically programmed to form mirror images of each other. If you bring your hands together in front of you, they will meet naturally in a vertical plane with palms together. If you move your left hand to your right, it will automatically turn over so that the palm faces down. If you move it to your left, the hand will naturally roll back the other way—that is, with the palm facing up. The right hand will do the same thing, although in reverse directions. The body's blueprint dictates that the hands move in this way, and the hands will always comply unless you make a conscious effort to stop them.

It is the control of the hands *within* the golf swing that enables the golfer to achieve a good swing by dropping into the slot. The hands exercise this control by imposing a learned skill on the natural tendency of the hands to turn over as you swing them across your body. If the body were designed differently and the dominant muscle groups which move the right arm across the body were attached to the inside of the upper arm—that is, in the armpit—it would be quite easy to pull the right arm into your side without rotating it. Golf would then be a much simpler game. In fact, the tendons of this dominant muscle group are attached to the outer front of the right arm, and these automatically cause the bone to rotate when the muscles pull on it. Demonstrate this to yourself. Standing up, extend your right arm to the right with your palm facing upwards and then swing it across the front of your body. As you do so, you will be able to observe the natural rotation of your arm which causes the hand to turn over into a vertical position and later into a palm-down position. Repeat the movement, this time keeping the hand palm-upwards. This is an unnatural movement, and you will be able to feel the substantial stress it puts on other parts of the body, yet it is the fundamental movement in the golf swing.

In the light of all this, let us look more closely at what the hands are required to do. In the backswing, the hands do automatically what good technique requires them to do—they roll over so that, at the top of the backswing, the right palm faces up. In the downswing, you have to prevent the hands from doing what comes naturally. Specifically, you must stop them turning back as early as they are genetically inclined to do. You must force your right hand to remain palm upwards for as long

CONTROL OF THE SWING

The sequence on these pages will be of special interest to left-handers. It shows one of the world's longest hitters, left-handed Gary Wise of Australia, in action. Here, he addresses the ball.

This photograph shows Wise's downswing, and demonstrates to perfection the flail action of the golf swing and how the wrists act as a free-hinge system. If Wise were attempting to "hit with his hands", the wrists would have straightened at this stage of his downswing, opening out the angle between his right arm and the shaft.

Wise is a big man, who by controlling his hands allows the smoothly moving mass of his arms to work for him in accordance with the laws of momentum, thereby generating the incredible distance he achieves.

It is not the speed at which his arms travel, but rather their great weight and the elimination of slack in his downswing that generate the distance Wise achieves.

Wise's follow-through from his powerful drive.

as you can. The reason you do this is to force your right elbow against your side, which is where it needs to be if you are going to drop into the slot. As I will explain in detail later, you can achieve this by locking your hands in a certain position at the very start of the downswing which prevents them from turning over too soon.

I touched before on the question of whether golf is a left-handed or a right-handed game. The learned skill that overrides genetic tendencies in the downswing is a right-handed skill. It's the right elbow that, contrary to what it would do naturally, has to remain pressed against the body. It's the right hand that, contrary to the instinctive impulse to push the club forward, has to pull back on it. It's the right forearm that, instead of moving naturally in a free arc, has to stay low. Clearly, the control of the golf swing resides in the right side of the body, which isn't so surprising when you consider that, in the average right-hander, the right side is more than 80 per cent dominant in motion control.

I have long pondered the question of why golf is so difficult for so many people. How often have you heard of a naturally talented person who has reached the top in other sports and who is successful in most areas of life yet who cannot play golf off 20? He may be extremely athletic and well co-ordinated, yet he has a second-rate golf swing. The reason, I suggest, lies in that part of the golf swing that is contrary to the normal genetic movement of the hands. Master this part of the golf swing and you will have mastered the golf swing itself.

TONY LEMA
This great player was a true master of the swing. Notice the exemplary position of his right arm.

THE SLOT

There are an awful lot of misconceptions about the role of the hands in golf. What are the hands? They are merely the ends of the arms. They can't do anything on their own. They can go only where the arms take them. Golf teachers will tell you that your hands have a vital task to perform in the downswing. It is the late release of the hands, they say, that accelerates the clubhead and gives your swing its striking power. Their belief in this is so strong that a controlled release of the hands is reckoned to be one of the fundamentals of the golf swing. But the theory is wrong. The hands are incapable of consciously performing such a manoeuvre in the fraction of a second available.

Yet, as we will see, the hands do have an absolutely vital role to play. It is no exaggeration to say they are the key to a successful golf swing. But first consider the basics of what you're trying to achieve when you swing the club down. Clearly, you seek to deliver the clubhead into the back of the ball with maximum force. To achieve this maximum force, the various forces generated in the downswing need to be acting in the same direction. To be more specific, you must bring your arms down in such a way that the forces of the downswing are aligned in the same plane before you strike the ball.

This is a technical description of something that mechanically is fairly simple. There is a law of physics underlying it all, which says that when two or more lever systems interact to create a force, the force will be greatest when the lever systems lie in a common plane. If you have ever used a crowbar you would know what this means in practice, for you can tell at once when you're using a crowbar whether you've got all your levers working in the one plane.

All good golfers can tell when they've got their levers working in the one plane, even if they know nothing about the mechanical principles involved. When they swing the club down, it somehow feels "right" to them, as if their forearms and wrists are slipping into place. Ben Hogan coined a term for it. He called it "the slot". When he was hitting correctly,

THE SLOT

he felt his arms sliding into this "slot" at the top of the downswing. What happened, in fact, was that his left forearm, his right forearm and the club began moving through what was virtually a common plane.

I do not know if Hogan himself really understood the mechanics of the slot. If he did, he must have worked it out himself, for until now no textbook has ever explained it. Many golfers know how to drop their hands into the slot, but they appear to have no understanding of what they are doing or why. I've read many supposedly authoritative writers discussing the matter and describing how you can drop into the slot if you have the club parallel with this or your wrists square with that. Obviously, they haven't an inkling of what the slot really is.

So how do you get your arms to fall into the slot? The answer to this question—and it is really the secret of the golf swing—is that you do it with your hands. **If you can concentrate on having your hands in the right position, all the other components of the downswing will fall into place of their own accord,** without your having to worry about them. It's like steering a car. The conscious act of turning the steering wheel in one direction sets in motion a whole series of mechanical movements within the car, the end result of which is that the wheels of the car turn in the same direction. You don't have to worry about these mechanical movements inside the car. You take it for granted that they'll happen automatically. All you need to think about is turning the steering wheel.

Consider the time problem again. The entire downswing takes two-tenths of a second, and since any conscious movement to control it would have to be initiated in the first half of the downswing, the time available to perform it can be no more than one-tenth of a second. This is only about half the normal human reaction time, so the controlling mechanism clearly cannot be a conscious, deliberate action after the downswing has begun. It can only be an action initiated at the start of the downswing.

It is generally accepted that at the top of the swing the arms should be rotated in such a way that the back of your left hand and the palm of your right hand are facing upwards. This position is advocated by nearly all the textbooks, and, for reasons I will explain later, they are correct in doing so. I like to drive the point home by telling golfers they must have their watches facing towards the sky. I say to them, "Let God tell the time," which seems to get the message across. There is one other thing

THE SLOT

you must do: cock your left wrist sideways, so that the thumb is almost at right angles to your forearm. To make sure you understand this, put this book down and grasp your left thumb with the two middle fingers of your right hand. If you then pull back on the left thumb, making sure your watch is facing upwards, you will have locked your hands in a position that closely approximates the one your hands need to be in at the start of the downswing.

We have now arrived at the heart of the matter. The only way you can control your hands in the downswing is by locking them into this special position *before* the downswing begins. By doing so, you effectively pre-program what the hands will do *during* the downswing. In particular, this positioning of the hands—right palm up, left wrist cocked—ensures that the hands drop into the slot. All you have to do as you swing the club down is concentrate on keeping your watch facing upwards for as long as possible (which is another way of saying keeping the palm of your right hand facing upwards). At the last moment, the forces acting on your hands will become so great that you will not be able to hold them in this position any longer, and the hands will roll over of their own accord and become square-on as you make contact. When we come to consider the downswing in detail, I will explain fully how this mechical pre-programming works.

Let us review the basics of the slot. To achieve maximum force with your golf swing, you need to have the three levers—that is, your two arms and the club—aligned as nearly as possible in the one plane. This is a simple, mechanical explanation of what Ben Hogan called the slot. How do you get your arms and the club aligned as nearly as possible in the one plane? You do it by jamming your right elbow against your side and keeping it there for as long as possible during the downswing. What happens here is that the right elbow acts as a pivot about which the right forearm can rotate. How do you force your right elbow against your side? The answer is to lock your hands in a position of right palm up and left palm down before the downswing begins—and to force your hands to maintain this unnatural position for as long as possible.

THE POWER OF
MENTAL IMAGERY

The golf swing, like all other human actions, is programmed in the mind before it is performed by the body. So to have the right golf swing, you must first have the right mental image of it. This is why understanding the mechanics of your golf swing is so important. What you see in your mind is what you will get.

Mental imagery has a big influence on how people perform in all sports, but it is of absolutely crucial importance in golf. Most other sports are reactive by nature. In a fraction of a second you must react to a moving tennis ball or football or basketball. In golf, you may have to walk 200 metres (200 yards) or more to the next shot, so you have plenty of time to fill your mind with fear and doubt. This is the reason so many top golfers run hot and cold. Take the case of the pro who shoots a round of 68 one day and 80 the next. Why has he shot 80? It isn't because he has lost any of his skill. His golf swing hasn't changed. It's because his mental image of what he's trying to do has changed. When a golfer is playing well, it's invariably because he can see clearly in his mind what he has to do. You sometimes hear golfers who have putted well say that they could "see" the line. In other words, they had a clear mental image of how and where they had to hit the ball. Conversely, if they don't putt well, it's almost certainly because they didn't have this clear mental image. Probably, their mind was scrambled by anxiety.

It's pointless worrying whether your right wrist is in the correct position or whether your left arm is straight if your mental imagery is wrong. **A golfer with an ordinary golf swing and the right mental image will play better golf than the golfer who has the perfect swing and the wrong mental image.** You will see examples of this on every course—golfers who are able to lob the ball 200 metres (200 yards) down the middle of the fairway, bunt it another 150 metres (150 yards) towards the green, chip it onto the green and have two putts into the hole. They've got their bogey, which is all they expected to get. They put no pressure on themselves, and, as a result, their minds are uncluttered.

THE POWER OF MENTAL IMAGERY

Let me give you a simple example of how destructive fear can be. If I asked you to walk across a plank lying on the ground, you would do it without a second thought. If I then laid the same plank across a chasm 500 metres (1600 feet) deep, you wouldn't walk across it at any price. Most golfers have experienced the same thing. On the practice range, they hit ball after ball with such power and accuracy that they begin to think that golf is the easiest game in the world. Next day they walk onto the golf course and find a lake in front of the first tee. On the practice range they had a clear image of what they had to do, but now the picture is blurred by fear, and the chances are they will hit into the lake. Often the fear is caused by bunkers. I have helped some golfers overcome this fear by telling them to aim at the bunker instead of the green. I say to them: "Hit it in the bunker, and then have some fun trying to get out." The interesting thing is that when they try to hit into the bunker they usually land on the green.

Like every other action we perform, the golf swing is actually a sequence of many small movements, each of which is a reaction to the movement that preceded it. If you focus your mind on these movements individually, you will throw the entire sequence of movements into disarray. You have time in the golf swing for only one conscious thought, and this thought must be devoted to the one conscious action you have to perform—namely, preventing the hands rolling over in the downswing as they are naturally inclined to do. The rest of the golf swing is pure reaction. You can't control it, so leave it alone—don't think about it. Keep your mind free.

Trust yourself to hit the ball the way you would like to hit it. Don't be intimidated by what you regard as the complexities of the golf swing. After all, you trust yourself to hit a nail with a hammer, and hitting a nail straight with a hammer is no less difficult than hitting a golf ball straight with a club. The two actions have a lot in common. The face of the hammer has to be raised through an arc and then brought down through an arc onto the head of the nail with power and extreme precision. You trust yourself to do this. You trust yourself to hold the hammer correctly, to get the angles right, to synchronize the various components of the downswing so as to deliver a hammer blow of maximum velocity. So trust yourself to hit the golf ball.

BALANCE

Balance is one of the keys to success in all sports, and it is of absolutely critical importance in golf. This has been said many times before, of course, but I know of very few golfers who understand the reasoning behind it. The explanation is quite simple. One of your subconscious mind's most powerful instincts is to maintain the balance of your body—in other words, to ensure you don't fall over and hurt yourself. This is a matter of self-preservation, so your brain gives it top priority. Conversely, although you may regard your golf swing as one of the most important things in your life, your subconscious mind regards it as being of no importance at all.

So if you come even close to losing your balance while swinging a golf club, perhaps by leaning too far forward or to the right, your subconscious mind will react instantly to the danger by taking over the control of your body from your conscious mind. It does this whether you like it or not. It wouldn't matter if you were lining up for a shot that could win the British Open—whenever your balance is threatened, your body's automatic balance-preserving mechanism will go into action, overriding whatever effort you may be making to control the club.

This function is so important that it pays to know a little about the neurology involved. The nervous system which carries information back to the brain gives different priorities to different kinds of messages. This happens at nerve junctions known as synapses. The synapses give immediate right of way to messages that the brain considers of top priority and delays others that are reckoned to be not so important—rather like switching all traffic lights at an intersection to red to let an ambulance drive through. Because balance is regarded by the brain as being of A1 importance, messages to the brain that have anything to do with balance will be given priority over any messages you send to your hands or arms to control your swing.

In the light of all this, every golfer must take care to ensure his balance is never in danger. The less your subconscious mind is called into action to maintain balance, the more you will be able to exercise acquired skills—which in this case means swinging the club successfully. A golfer's body may be likened to a tall pole kept upright by ropes on all sides. If the pole is perfectly vertical, it will stand upright on its own. If it leans to one side, ropes on the other side will have to be pulled to prevent it toppling. The further it leans, the harder the ropes will have to be pulled. It is the same with the golfer. The more his balance is threatened, the more various muscles will automatically be brought into action to prevent him falling. The significance of this is that some of these muscles are also used in the golf swing. If they are already engaged by the balance mechanism, clearly they cannot be nearly as effective in helping to swing the club.

There is one thing about balance that every golfer should be aware of: your hips and head always move to counterbalance each other. If your head moves in one direction, your hips will move in the opposite direction, and vice versa. You can demonstrate this for yourself simply by standing up and leaning your head forwards or backwards or to one side. What happens is that the body adjusts itself automatically to keep its centre of gravity above your feet. Because the golfer leans his head beyond the line of his toes, as he is supposed to do, his hips and rump move backwards to counterbalance it.

This is the reason for the golfer's "squat"—the name given to the familiar crouch that top golfers drop into as they swing the club. The weight of the golfer's arms and club as they swing around in front of the body, plus the centrifugal force they exert, compel the golfer to stick out his rump further to balance them, which naturally lowers his height. The effect of this can be pronounced. For example, measurements I have done indicate that at impact Jack Nicklaus's head is only 158 centimetres (5 feet 2 inches) above the ground, that Arnold Palmer's is 147 centimetres (4 feet 10 inches), and Lee Trevino's only 137 centimetres (4 feet 6 inches). This "crouch" during the golf swing is not deliberate, of course. Rather, it is an involuntary movement to maintain balance.

Even to a casual observer it is obvious that some golfers tend to have more upright swings while others have flatter swings. **The angle of the swing, upright or flat, is really a function of balance.** In the course of the golf swing the golfer moves the club and his arms (which can weigh as much as 13 kilograms, or 28 pounds, between them) across and above his body, and this naturally has a dramatic effect on his balance. If you

BALANCE

study the good players, you will find that at the top of their swing they invariably have their hands above or slightly in front of their heels. But this is about all they do have in common. Whether their swing is upright or flat is determined by their height, their body shape and the distance they stand from the ball. Ben Hogan, who swung the club on a very flat plane, was 173 centimetres (5 feet 8 inches) tall and stood as much as 90 centimetres (35 inches) from the ball. Jack Nicklaus (see the frontispiece) who has an upright swing, is 178 centimetres (5 feet 10 inches) tall and stands 74 centimetres (29 inches) from the ball, fully 16 centimetres (about 6 inches) closer than Hogan. Other players also exemplify this. The photographs between pages 16 and 17 showed clearly that Nick Faldo, who is tall, stands much closer to the ball than Lee Trevino, who is 170 centimetres (5 feet 7 inches) tall.

THE GRIP

The importance of the grip has been vastly overrated in golfing lore. The grip doesn't contribute anything positive to the golf swing. All it does is attach the club to the ends of your arms. Nothing more. For reasons of mechanics, the more the grip allows your hands and wrists to approximate a single hinge, the better. Provided your grip creates this free hinge, it does not really matter how you hold the club.

THE METHOD

For your hands and wrists to act effectively as a single hinge, there is just one requirement—the hands must be as close together on the club as possible. This means that you will have to interlock or overlap the fingers of your two hands in some way, although precisely how you do this is entirely up to you. Your first priority is your golf swing, not your grip. So, simply hold the club in any way that feels comfortable and concentrate on mastering your swing. Later, having mastered your swing, you may decide to make small adjustments to the way you are holding the club.

There are two other points of technique you need concern yourself with. First, make sure the butt of the club projects slightly beyond the heel of your left hand. If it doesn't—if it is buried somewhere in the palm of your left hand—you will not feel in control of the club, and this itself can cause problems. Second, don't grip the club with the forefinger and thumb of the right hand. They should be relaxed and allowed to hang free, out of the grip.

THE MECHANICS

Over the years millions of words have been devoted to the subject of the grip, and, unfortunately for golfers, most have been wrong. Theories on the grip are generally based on a false premise—namely, that the hands have a positive role to play in hitting the ball. So golfers everywhere have been taught to the hold the club so they can hit the ball with their hands.

THE GRIP

As we have seen, this is impossible. By gripping the club, you are merely connecting the club to your arms. It is unfortunate that the term "grip" is used at all, for it suggests something that is positive and technical. It would be much better to call it, simply, "holding" the club.

Otherwise, hold the club any way you like, but bear in mind two things. The first is that you should have your hands as close together as possible. This isn't because it looks better or feels comfortable. There is a principle of physics involved. If you are transferring energy through a system of levers, you will do it more efficiently if each lever has a free hinge—that is, a single point of pivot. So what you must try to do with the golf club is have it swinging on a free hinge at the end of your arms. The closer you have your hands together, the nearer you will come to creating this free hinge at your wrists. In particular, you need to have the two middle fingers of the right hand, which actually hold the club, as close as possible to the left hand, so that you end up with six fingers (the two middle fingers of the right hand and the four fingers of the left) as one unit. It is this six-finger unit that then holds the club. This is the only logical reason for interlocking or overlapping your fingers. It has nothing to do with "bonding the hands"—a phrase coaches have liked to use. For reasons I will explain later, you should keep the right forefinger and thumb out of the grip entirely—let them hang loose and free.

The second thing to bear in mind is this: the grip you begin with ought to be the grip you end up with at the moment of impact if you are hitting the ball with the clubface square to the ball. To express this another way, choose whichever grip is easiest to return to just before you hit the ball. This is where many golfers go wrong. They read a coaching book written by Jack Nicklaus or some other champion and they follow his advice on gripping the club right down to the last finger. The book says, "Thou shalt grip the club this way," and they obey. What they should be doing is experimenting to find which grip suits them personally, given the requirement that they must bring their hands back to that position at the bottom of the downswing. Far from being a matter of rigid technique, as it is generally presented, the grip is actually the most do-as-you-please part of the golf swing. Many of the top golfers have had highly unconventional grips.

I draw attention elsewhere to the fact that golfers can learn a number of things from the simple act of swinging a hammer. Perhaps the most important of them is the fact that hammering a nail is a pure lever

THE GRIP

action. Take hold of a hammer or hammer-like object and demonstrate this to yourself. You will see that the familiar "flick of the wrist" which whips the hammer head onto the nail is not a movement *by* the wrist at all. Rather, the hammer is pulled over in a lever action by the last three fingers of the right hand, acting on a fulcrum provided by the grip of the forefinger and the thumb. This is clearly shown in the photograph opposite page 40. It is the momentum of the hammer head generated by this lever action that causes the wrist to "flick", acting merely as a hinge.

Unfortunately, the same thing can happen in the golf swing. I say "unfortunately", because if you make it possible for the clubhead to whip through like the head of a hammer and uncock the wrist, it will do so too early, throwing the clubhead out and causing the right elbow to fly and the right hand to roll over. The golfer's aim must be to keep the wrist cocked back for as long as possible in the downswing. How does he prevent the club whipping through prematurely like a hammer? He does it by spreading and relaxing the forefinger and thumb so that they cannot act as a pivot. In other words, he does not grip the club at all with the forefinger and thumb. None of the great players do once they have reached the top of the backswing. If you study photographs of them, you will see that this is true. So get rid of the idea that you can in some way hit with the hands, and don't take a strong grip on the club as if you intended to. Open up the right forefinger and thumb—let them hang relaxed and loose. If you do, your golf swing will gain in freedom.

Once you have found a grip that enables you to hit freely and far, don't meddle with the basics of it. There have been golfers who, after coming to me for help, began hitting the ball with a power and consistency they had never dreamed of—yet kept hitting the ball to one side of the target. Many golfers would try to rectify this by adjusting their grip. My strong advice was not to change their grip or their swing in any way. After all, they now had a mechanism that was functioning superbly. They were hitting the ball further than ever before. If they were hitting, say, 20 metres (20 yards) to the left, why not simply aim 20 metres (20 yards) to the right? Or, better still, why not turn the clubface around a couple of degrees—without changing the grip itself—so that it was slightly open to the target? I call this "dialling a shot". You experiment by turning the shaft around in either direction (which, of course, results in the clubface striking the ball at different angles) until you find yourself hitting the ball where you want it to go. Fix on this as your grip.

THE GRIP

There is another tip I would like to offer here. Many golfers break a cardinal rule of good technique by having their hands behind the ball at the moment of impact. A simple way to correct this fault is to close the clubface slightly when you address the ball. What you are doing here is playing a trick on your mind. To compensate for the fact that the clubface is closed, you feel compelled to move your hands forward. In other words, you are being forced to experience what you ought to be doing naturally. After you have done this a number of times and know what needs to be done, turn the clubface back to its normal plane.

Good golfers are able to vary the direction they hit the ball by making slight alterations to the grip itself. By all means adjust your grip as the need arises, but don't make the mistake of picking up the club in some preconceived manner and trying to force the rest of your golf swing to accommodate it. Adjust your natural grip, but don't adopt an unnatural grip and try to fashion your swing around it. Learn to swing the club first. Worry about the grip later.

POSTURE

Your aim when you address the ball must be to adopt a posture that will allow you to turn freely as you take back the club. To do this, it is essential to avoid engaging the wrong muscles when you address the ball—that is, muscles that will oppose and impede the muscles doing the turning. The "wrong" muscles in this case are those in the front of your body. If you can avoid engaging them, the muscles in your back responsible for turning your body will be able to operate without interference.

THE METHOD

Do not make the cardinal mistake of lowering your head towards your chest as you prepare to address the ball, for this will engage muscles in the front of your body all the way down from your neck to your thighs. Indeed, the mere intention of lowering your head like this will trigger these frontal muscles. Instead, keep your chin up and incline your whole

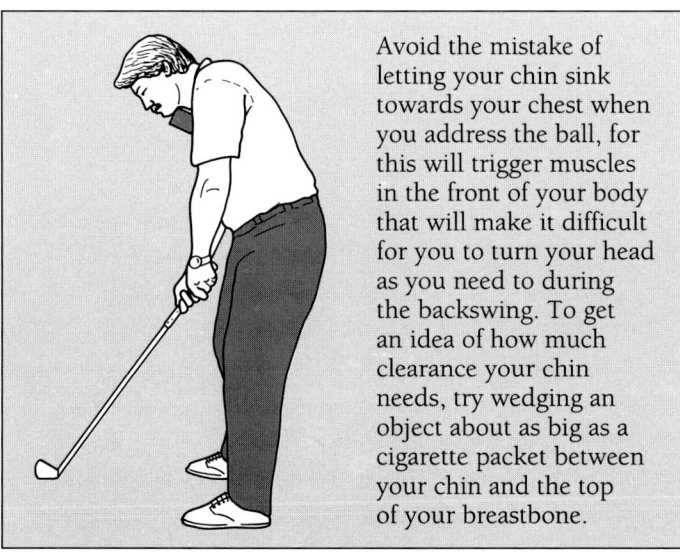

Avoid the mistake of letting your chin sink towards your chest when you address the ball, for this will trigger muscles in the front of your body that will make it difficult for you to turn your head as you need to during the backswing. To get an idea of how much clearance your chin needs, try wedging an object about as big as a cigarette packet between your chin and the top of your breastbone.

upper body forward from the waist, making sure that you maintain plenty of clearance between your chin and your chest. One way to confirm that you are doing this correctly is to wedge something the size of a cigarette packet, end-on, between your chin and your chest as you lean forwards over the ball, for this is roughly the amount of clearance you need to maintain.

Once you have inclined your upper body in the way I have described, you can begin to shuffle your feet into position. Most golfers bend their knees quite naturally, for this improves their balance and makes it easier for them to turn. Apart from allowing your spine to bend slightly to the right (which makes it easier to swing the club down in the right plane), try to keep it as straight as possible.

Here is a common mistake to avoid: **do not straighten your left arm when you address the ball.** By doing so, you trigger muscles in the left shoulder and upper arm that make it extremely difficult to swing the left arm across your body in the backswing. Instead, the left arm should be relaxed—and therefore slightly bent—when you grip the club. Try the two postures and see the difference for yourself. First, extend a relaxed left arm in front of you as if you were addressing a ball. If the arm is relaxed, it will naturally be slightly bent. Now swing it as if you were taking back a club. It will move freely and easily. Try the same thing again, this time locking your left arm straight. At once, you will feel muscles tense in the left shoulder and behind the upper arm. If you now try to swing the straight left arm across your body, the movement will be extremely restricted.

THE MECHANICS

A good golfing posture is one that is balanced and comfortable and that allows you to turn freely. Before examining what makes for good posture, however, let us study some of the more obvious posture faults. At the top of the list is the habit golfers have of letting their chins drop into their chests. It is by a long way the most common flaw in golfing posture, and my guess is that 90 per cent of golfers do it to some degree.

When a golfer addresses the ball, his first inclination is to look at it by lowering his eyes. In other words, he lowers his head *before* he inclines his body forward. Automatically, as he does this, his chin drops into his chest, triggering muscles in the front of his neck and, in turn, the muscles in the front of his torso and legs. As a result, it becomes difficult to turn his head as he needs to during the backswing. If muscles on one side of the body are engaged, the opposing muscles on the other side of the body (in this case, the muscles that turn the head) will not countermand them. So if you've got the muscles of your chest and abdomen engaged, the muscles of the back won't override them.

The trick is to put the right muscles into action, and fortunately there is a simple means of ensuring this. Instead of lowering your eyes, look ahead and then lean forwards from the hips until you are looking straight down at the ball.

This manoeuvre not only prevents your chin from becoming locked into the front of your body, it also has the effect of engaging the muscles of your back, which means that you are ideally positioned to begin turning your head and shoulders as you begin the backswing. It achieves one other thing. By keeping your head up—that is, clear of your chest—you won't find yourself lifting your head when you swing the club. This lifting of the head is actually an automatic adjustment of the body's balancing mechanism, which is reacting to the head being bent down. This leads to amazing confusion among coaches and their pupils. You hear the coach telling the golfer to keep his head down, but the more the golfer tries to keep his head *down*, the more it tends to come up. Ironically, the more you try to keep your head up—that is, away from your chest—the better you will keep it down during the downswing.

Once you have inclined your upper body forwards, you can begin shuffling your feet into the correct position. So the order of movement is head first, feet second, since where you stand will naturally be dictated by the position of your head.

All golfers stand with knees bent, although some bend them more than others. (Those who bend them a lot often do so simply because their clubs are too short.) It is sometimes said you should bend your knees because it is easier to turn on bent knees than on straight ones, and to a marginal degree this is true. But a much more important reason is balance. The primary lines of balance between the legs and the upper body are situated in the bones of the thighs, while the secondary lines lie in the shins. If the knees are apart and bent, these primary lines will point outwards, which effectively means you will have a wider brace on which to move. In other words, you will have the same balance as if your feet were wider apart.

By having your knees bent, you are also better able to resist the

THE GRIP

When the thumb and forefinger of the right hand are in the correct, relaxed position, as shown here, the right hand is prevented from performing a natural hammer action with the club, which would cause the wrists to release prematurely, resulting in an early hit.

The middle fingers of the right hand—the two that grip the club—and the last three fingers of the left hand need to be as close together as possible to form a single pivot point, allowing the wrists to act as a free hinge.

To swing a hammer, the last three fingers pull on the butt, and the hammer swings forward on the pivot provided by the forefinger and thumb. If this happens in the golf swing, however, the clubhead will whip through too early. The forefinger and thumb must be kept out of the grip, and allowed to hang loose and free.

This is the two-handed or baseball grip—and it is the wrong way to grip a golf club. This type of grip allows the right hand to be too dominant in the swing.

POSTURE
Pages 38-41

At address, the golfer's posture should be relaxed and comfortable. The left elbow is slightly bent, indicating that the arm is hanging in its natural rest position.

In the correct posture, the stance is relaxed and the spine straight.

This is an example of incorrect posture. The chin is tucked into the chest, the legs are straight, and the spine is humped, restricting movement and rotation of the spine. Sooner or later a stance of this kind will almost certainly lead to back injury.

Greg Norman's posture shows knees well bent and apart. "Just stand there and keep your knees the same and everything automatically turns, your shoulders turning on the same plane as your hips."

THE STANCE
Pages 42-6

The two photographs taken from above show the correct position at address and impact. From this position, the player is able to hit downwards on the ball. In the side view at impact, note how the golfer is holding his body back from the ball to allow the left arm and the shaft to be fully extended.

POSTURE

centrifugal forces in the club that tend to pull you forwards. Think of the hammer-thrower. Swinging the hammer around generates strong centrifugal forces in the hammer. The harder he swings it around, the more he bends his knees.

So far we have looked at the head and the legs. What of the back? Here, we come to a fundamental of golf posture: keep your backbone straight throughout the backswing. (I am referring here, of course, to the spine as viewed from the back. Obviously, the spine has a natural curvature when viewed from the side.) Again, it is a matter of making sure you don't engage muscles that interfere with the muscles you need to use. When the spine is straight, it is in its natural, resting position. When it is bent, muscles in the back automatically go into action to cope with the distortion, and these interfere with the activity of muscles you are using in the golf swing.

One minor qualification must be added to this. It is accepted that the clubhead should travel from inside the target line (an imaginary line running through the ball to the target) out to the ball, rather than from outside in. It becomes easier to do this if you incline both your spine and your head a little towards the right, because the club swinging around the inclined spine is much more likely to stay inside the target line.

The main reason so many golfers swing from outside in is that they are trying to keep their body behind the ball, believing they will hit it further that way. What they ought to be doing is positioning themselves *above* the ball so that they can hit downwards on it. If you study photographs of the top pros in action, you will find that their right ear invariably ends up over their right ankle at the top of the backswing. In other words, contrary to "orthodox" teaching, their head does move to the right. Then, as the downswing begins, their entire body moves to the left. What they are doing here is moving to position themselves *above* the ball to hit downwards on it. If you stay behind the ball, you can't hit downwards on it. Even to reach the ball from such a position, you have to swing out and around, which is probably what 95 per cent of the world's golfers do.

THE STANCE

The purpose of the stance is simple enough. You need to position yourself in relation to the ball so that you can hit it with maximum power and precision. There are a number of considerations that determine precisely where you should place your feet, but the most important of them is the necessity of being able to hit *downwards* on the ball. So when you choose your stance you must position yourself so that you will be *above* the ball, not behind it, when you make contact.

THE METHOD

The first thing to do is to clear your mind of the many misconceptions you probably have about the golf stance. Forget the idea that you have to have your feet at certain angles—the right foot square to the target line and so on. Simply place your feet in whichever position feels most natural and comfortable. For nine out of ten golfers, this will mean standing with both feet slightly turned out in the ordinary way. If you are naturally pigeon-toed, however, and feel more comfortable with your feet turned in, then by all means adopt this as your stance.

All the other questions—how close you should stand to the ball, whether you should stand with the ball closer to your left foot than your right, and so on—can be answered only by personal experimentation. So work out your correct stance by trial and error, but keep in mind that your right foot, not your left, should be the main point of reference when you are positioning your feet in relation to the ball. **Be careful to avoid standing with the ball too far forward—that is, too close to the left foot.**

Here is a simple method of working out what your own stance should be. Without looking at the ground, swing a club backwards and forwards as you would in a normal golf stroke, gradually lowering the swing until the club begins to strike the ground and takes a divot. If your positioning was correct, the ball would have been between one and two centimetres (between three-eighths and three-quarters of an inch) to the right of the back of the divot. If you then mark the spot with a tee, you will be able to see clearly where it is in relationship to your left and right foot. This will vary from club to club. The general rule is that the higher the club number, the closer your right foot needs to be to the ball.

THE MECHANICS

The first thing to consider about the stance is the alignment of the feet. According to orthodox teaching, you should stand with your right foot at right angles to the target line and your left foot slightly splayed. Ben Hogan was very particular on this latter point. He stipulated that the left foot should be splayed one quarter of a turn to the left. Such theories have no logical basis whatever within the laws of physics, so disregard them.

Before you make a final choice about where you point your feet, however, consider this fact. The direction you point your feet has a big effect on your ability to turn at the hips. This can be demonstrated by a simple experiment. Stand with your feet parallel with each other and twist your torso as far as you can towards the right. Now turn your left foot so that it is at right angles to your right foot, and then try twisting your torso to the right again. You will find you cannot turn it nearly so far as before, the reason being that when you turned your left foot 90 degrees to the left, you effectively turned your body by half that amount, or 45 degrees, to the left, and used up 45 degrees of your spine's capacity for rotation. The same thing happens (to a lesser extent, of course) whenever you have your feet at different angles to the toe line.

Having your right foot square to the target line, as many teachers advocate, offers no mechanical advantage at all. Those who recommend it say it enables a golfer to wind the spring of his spine tighter. But muscles aren't elastic—they cannot be stretched like rubber bands.

Many great golfers have splayed both feet in the way I suggest. Sam Snead certainly did. Jack Nicklaus doesn't always have his right foot splayed, yet he is on record as saying that if he wants to hit the ball a long way, he turns his right foot out, the idea being that this allows greater freedom in his backswing.

The next thing to consider is how you position yourself laterally in relation to the ball. Should the ball be directly in front, a little to the left, or a little to the right? The average golfer invariably makes the mistake of positioning himself so that the ball is too far to the left. What he's trying to do, without realizing it, is to get behind the ball, because

THE STANCE

he thinks that the more he can get behind it, the better he'll hit it. One harmful consequence of this is that there is a tendency to turn the head to the left as you address the ball, which causes complications when you have to turn your head to the right at the start of the backswing.

The key to the whole question is that the golfer's body pivots mainly on the right leg, not the left. The right leg anchors the golfer for most of the golf swing. It is only in the latter stages of the follow-through that the body pivots on the left leg. Yet nearly all the masters of the game have advocated placing the ball in relation to the left leg. If the body is pivoting on the right leg, clearly the ball should be placed in relation to that leg, so that you can comfortably move forward and hit *down* on it. If the ball is too far from your right leg, you won't be able to reach it comfortably and, inevitably, you'll have to hit at it from outside in. The conclusion from all this is clear: when you take your stance, gauge your position by the ball's relationship to your right leg, not the left.

The other important question is how you should position your feet relative to the target line. The generally accepted view is that you should adopt a slightly closed stance (right foot back) when you are using a driver or long iron and a slightly open stance (left foot back) when you are using shorter irons—that is, from about number four downwards. In other words, the more loft there is on the club, the more you pull your left foot back. If this idea works for you, by all means use it. **Provided you can deliver the clubhead with force squarely into the back of the ball, it doesn't really matter where you stand.**

How far apart should your feet be? Again, there is no hard and fast rule to follow. The longer the iron, the further apart you will need to place your feet to maintain good balance, but otherwise you are free to do as you please. My general advice is to keep your stance as narrow as possible while still maintaining good balance.

How close to the ball should you place your feet? Balance is the determining factor here. The human body is like a beer bottle turned upside down—staying upright is no simple matter for it. The body is kept upright by an automatic mechanism which makes use of opposing muscles on opposite sides of the body. If you lean your body in one direction, muscles on the other side will try to pull it back. The further you lean, the harder they pull. What the balance mechanism try to do is to return your head to a position above the feet.

What does all this mean for the golfer? It means he has to place

THE STANCE

his feet in such a way that he can swing easily and freely without causing the subconscious brain to think his balance is in danger. It means he must keep his chin in front of his toes throughout the golf swing, which in turn means he must have his rump sticking out slightly behind his heels.

For as long as people have played golf there have been arguments over this question of how far you should stand from the ball. The top golfers obviously don't agree on it. Jack Nicklaus appears to stand about 74 centimetres (29 inches) from the ball, as measured from the centre of the ball to the toe line, which is closer than any other top golfer I have measured. Ben Hogan, a shorter man, stood as much as 90 centimetres (35 inches) from the ball. There is a huge difference here, yet you can't say one of these great golfers was right and the other wrong. It all comes down to balance.

Consider the two golfers just mentioned. Nicklaus happens to have unusually short and solid arms. Hogan's arms were solid, too, but proportionally longer. The point has been made before that arms are actually quite heavy objects, weighing as much as 13 kilograms (28 pounds) between them, so when you move them about your body you are shifting a sizeable amount of weight. In the light of this, let us now examine Ben Hogan's stance. Hogan had a flat swing which went around his body. During his backswing he was effectively shifting about 13 kilograms (28 pounds) of mass from in front of his point of balance—in this case, the arches of his feet—to just behind his heels, which means that to maintain perfect balance he had to stand further from the ball.

Nicklaus, on the other hand, has an upright swing—he tends to move the weight of his arms above his heels rather than behind them. To maintain balance, therefore, he has to stand closer to the ball. If Nicklaus stood as far back from the ball as Hogan did, he would fall on his face when he swung the club. If Hogan had stood as close to the ball as Nicklaus does, he would have fallen over backwards. The lesson from all this is simply to stand as far back from the ball as you need to stand to keep good balance, the general rule being that the further you take the club behind you in the backswing, the further you must stand from the ball.

Here is an exercise you may well find rewarding. Let us imagine you have teed the ball and are ready to hit it with the driver. Now, instead of addressing the ball on the tee, address an imaginary ball 8 to 10

THE STANCE

centimetres (3 to 4 inches) closer to you. In other words, choose a stance and organize your balance as if you were going to hit this imaginary ball. Having done so, take the club back normally and then try to hit the ball on the tee. I would not be surprised if you hit it with a power, freedom and control you have never experienced before. Gone is your old, weak, outside-in slap at the ball. What you have done here is allowed enough room between your spine and the ball for a full swing with an extended left arm.

This is actually an essential of the downswing: your spine must be pulled back far enough from the ball to allow you to hit it with arms and club shaft fully extended—that is, the top of the left arm, or shoulder socket, must remain in front of the torso prior to impact. If the spine is too close to the ball, the top of the left arm, or shoulder socket, will inevitably pull back too early. This causes excessive and premature shoulder spin. In the exercise you have just completed, you cannot hit from outside in for the simple reason that, even if you wanted to, you couldn't reach far enough to get outside the ball line.

Whenever I suggest placing the ball like this, beyond the toe of the club, it is only as an experiment to let golfers experience the feeling of free extension. But many golfers who try it find the results of the experiment so marvellous that they adopt it permanently. One extra advantage is that it automatically slows the start of the downswing. You cannot any longer just lift up the club and slash out and down. Instead, you feel a need to extend outwards and reach further, and the very need to do this causes you to slow down.

In case you shrink from anything that has not been tried and tested, let me tell you that Bobby Jones addressed the ball in this way throughout his career—that is, with the toe of his club just inside the ball. Jones won thirteen majors in a remarkably short time. It was good enough for him to use and should be good enough for you to try.

THE BACKSWING

The backswing is a purely preparatory movement. Its purpose is to get the club, the arms, the torso and, most important of all, the hands into the correct position from which to begin the downswing. Provided the golfer ends up in this correct position at the top of the backswing, it doesn't really matter how he gets there. This is why the backswings of the top players vary enormously. Their backswings do have one—and only one—thing in common. They give the golfer enough time and enough room to move into the position he needs to be in before the downswing begins.

There are four essentials. First, the hands and wrists must be locked in the precise position I referred to in the chapter on the slot (on pages 27-8), which ensures that they drop into the slot at the start of the downswing. Secondly the palm of the right hand must be facing upwards. If it isn't, muscles behind and above the right shoulder will be engaged, and this will interfere with the start of the downswing. The third essential is to move your head to the right and slightly backwards, so that the right ear ends up over the right ankle, and the fourth is to end up with your weight over your right heel. So the key to the backswing is: take the club back in any way you choose, provided you end up with your hands locked in the correct position (to be described later), with the palm of your right hand uppermost, and with your right ear over your right ankle and your weight over your right heel.

THE METHOD

The backswing is really a movement to the right. Most golfers are so preoccupied with having to hit the ball to the left that mentally and physically they are incapable of moving with freedom in the opposite direction. The way to overcome this is to *begin* the backswing by turning your head and your eyes to the right. This not only makes it easier then for your shoulders to turn, but it creates in your mind a mental image of moving to the right. Once your brain has registered this mental image,

THE BACKSWING

you will find that your backswing becomes wonderfully free.

After turning your head to the right, begin taking the club back and turning your body, making sure you do both together. In particular, avoid taking the club back before you have turned your body, because this causes your hips to sway to the right, one of the worst and most common faults of the backswing. You can accomplish this by keeping both arms extended and rotating them in unison with your shoulders. In practice, this means that the triangle formed by your arms and the line of your shoulders as you address the ball will remain almost intact as you rotate your shoulders to the right. Also, take care not to let your wrists drop as you take the club back, because this will trigger muscles in your forearm that will impede the backswing. In other words, keep the clubhead higher than the plane of your arms.

Thereafter, your only concern will be to get your hands into the required position at the top of the backswing—that is, with your right palm facing upwards and your left wrist cocked sideways. To simulate this manoeuvre, grip your left thumb with the two middle fingers of the right hand, as if you were gripping the club, and pretend to take the club back. As you do this, push with the left thumb against the two fingers of your right hand. Automatically, this will force your hands into the desired position at the top of the backswing.

Another way to simulate this movement is to imagine you have a plate of biscuits resting on the palm of your right hand. I then tell golfers: "Pass the biscuits around"—in other words, turn and pretend to offer the biscuits to people on your right. This movement of your right hand closely approximates the real one it needs to make in the backswing.

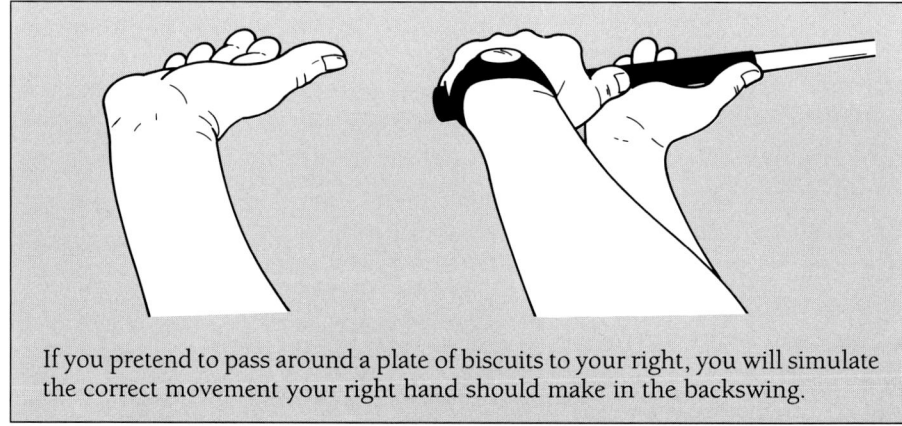

If you pretend to pass around a plate of biscuits to your right, you will simulate the correct movement your right hand should make in the backswing.

THE BACKSWING

THE MECHANICS

I use the term "backswing" reluctantly, because it isn't really a backswing at all. It's an inside-and-up swing. The clubhead doesn't go straight back. It is moved inside the target line and then lifted up. Similarly, the downswing is really a down-and-out swing, because that is the path the club actually follows. So when you come upon the word "backswing" here, remember that it is only a name—not a description of a movement.

A movement to the right and backwards

As we have seen, the head does not have to remain rigidly still. You may and should turn your head to the right—and you should do it before you start to raise the club. There are several reasons for this, and one is psychological. Here's an illustration of what I mean. Imagine you were standing between two logs, and I told you to get ready to jump sideways over one of them. This would no doubt seem quite simple. But if I then suddenly told you to jump sideways over the other log, you would probably be unable to move. Mentally and physically if you've primed yourself to move in one direction, you can't instantly move in the other.

It's the same with most golfers. Their objective is to hit the ball to the left, so they prime themselves to move in that direction, and lock muscles into position accordingly. Many also position themselves too far behind the ball as they address it and then turn their head slightly to the left so that they can focus their vision on the bottom half of the back of the ball. Thus their body is set left and their head (the centre of their automatic balancing mechanism) is turned slightly to the left, triggering balance to the left. Small wonder that they have difficulty in turning to the right in the backswing!

The key to the backswing is that it is initially a movement to the right, and you will perform it more fluently and naturally if your attention is directed to the right—that is, if you think backwards, not forwards. Turning your face to the right is a simple way to create this mental image. A number of top golfers do this, Jack Nicklaus among them. If you study the golfers who turn their body furthest and with the greatest freedom, you will find that they are the ones who turn their face furthest to the right at or before the start of the backswing. Some don't only turn their head to the right—they look to the right, too.

Turning your head before the backswing frees your shoulders to turn. The earlier the head is turned, and the further it is turned, the more freely the shoulders and hips will turn. Stand up and experiment with this, holding your hands together as if they were gripping a club. You will see at once that it is true.

I said before that the head moves back a little as well as to the right, which it must do, of course, if the right ear is to end up over the right ankle. In fact, the whole spine moves back a little during the backswing—that is, towards the heel line—and it is held back in this position during the downswing to allow the arms to be fully extended.

The head is a key item in the body's apparatus. It is the top of the spine and it holds the centres of balance. It is the one part of the body to which all other parts relate. Watch someone walking down a corridor and turning to go through a door. The head will always be the first part of the body to turn. The rest of the body follows. This is what should happen in your golf swing.

The eye *off* the ball

It is a physical fact that you don't actually *see* the ball when you hit it. The eyes undergo a dramatic change in visual focus as the head moves about during the golf swing. At best, you see the ball as a white blur on a green background, which raises the question: why concentrate your focus on the ball when you take the club back if you have no hope at all of focusing on it when you swing the club down? Nobody is going to steal the ball when you're not looking. All the golfer really needs is a vague reassurance that the ball is still there. I have gone so far as to advise some to avoid looking at the ball entirely during the backswing and downswing. I tell them their brain will remember where the ball was. The interesting thing is that when they don't look at the ball, they usually hit it superbly.

By focusing your vision intensely, you create tensions in the body which inhibit your muscular freedom in the golf swing. Conversely, if you don't stare at the ball, you can hit with more freedom. Just keep a vague eye on the ball as you turn your head a little to the right in the backswing. Your backswing and your downswing will thus become wonderfully free and natural.

Taking the club back

Certain champion golfers have come to the conclusion that if they move the clubhead back along the target line and keep the clubface looking at the ball for the first 30 centimetres (12 inches) or so of the backswing, this will somehow induce the clubhead to return along the same path to the ball in the downswing. This is merely wishful thinking. The brain cannot pre-program reverse movements of this kind, for we're dealing here with separate sets of muscles: those that take the club back and those that swing the club down. In any case, if your downswing is correct you will bring the club down in an arc from inside the target line, so it is geometrically impossible for you to swing the club along the target line for the final 30 centimetres (12 inches) before impact.

Thus, the notion that you can return the clubhead to the ball by taking it back along the target line defies logic. Yet the exercise is not entirely pointless. By taking the clubhead back along the target line as far as this, the golfer forces his left hand to move beyond his right shoulder, and by doing so he gives himself a little extra time and space to get his right arm locked into position before the downswing begins.

Lifting the club up

The golfer's number-one concern here must be to ensure that the biceps muscle in his right arm, not the muscles behind and above the shoulder, do the lifting. The reason: if you engage these muscles in your back, you will interfere with your downswing. This may sound a rather minor and obscure point, but it is actually very important. In practice, make sure you do *not* start to raise your upper right arm before the right forearm has begun to bend upwards at the elbow. Your intention here is to avoid engaging the trapezius, a big muscle behind and above the shoulder. Just the intention of raising your right arm before it is bent at the elbow will subconsciously trigger the trapezius. If the trapezius is engaged, it will automatically raise the right shoulder, resulting in a curvature of the spine and causing the head to tilt to the left. Thus, everything you ought to have avoided in the backswing will have happened.

So this premature lifting of the upper arm is what you must avoid at all costs. Provided you do avoid it, you can take the club back in almost any way you like. Virtually any backswing that has the right arm bending at the elbow before being raised at the shoulder is a satisfactory backswing. As outlined before, the best way of ensuring this is to preserve the triangle formed by your arms and the line of your shoulders until well into the backswing. When you are addressing the ball with your arms extended forwards, the triangle points down at the ground in front of you. For the first half of the backswing your arms should remain extended and move in unison with your turning shoulders. In other words, the triangle that previously was pointing at the ground in front of you has turned around so that it is pointing at the ground about a metre (3 feet) to the right of your right foot. From this position, your arms can fold easily at the elbows and you can raise the club in a simple, natural movement which is actually identical to the movement you would make to swing an axe over your shoulder while chopping wood.

Control by the hands

The hands are the prime movers in the backswing. By positioning them correctly, you can make the other parts of the backswing fall into place. Here is a simple way of tracking the movement the hands need to make. Begin by extending your hands in front of you with palms together, prayer-style, and both thumbs uppermost. This represents the position you adopt as you address the ball. Now simulate the start of the backswing by moving the hands to the right, keeping the arms extended. As you do so, the hands begin rolling over so that the palm of the right hand starts to face upwards. This rolling of the hands will happen automatically—*provided you have avoided the cardinal error of raising your right upper arm.* As the hands roll over, the right arm begins to bend at the elbow and your hands are raised to the level of your shoulder. At this point, which represents the top of the backswing, the watch on your left wrist should be pointing directly upwards. See the photographs of the backswing in the colour section between pages 56 and 57.

By rolling your right hand over so that the palm is facing upwards, you ensure that when you come to lift the club the biceps does most of the lifting. Why is this important? The reason is that if your right palm is allowed to face even partly downwards while you're raising the club, the muscles of the back and the arm and shoulder—specifically, the trapezius and brachialis—will be triggered into action automatically to complete the lifting process. As we have seen, this will raise the right shoulder, curve the spine and tilt the head to the left. Moreover, if the trapezius is engaged, it won't be able to release the right side in time for the downswing, forcing you to come over and outside the ball.

A simple experiment will allow you to feel the difference between what is right and wrong here. Hold your right hand in front of you with the palm facing upwards and then raise it to shoulder height. The movement will feel simple and easy, because it is being performed by the muscles designed by nature to perform the action, mainly the biceps and triceps. Perform the lifting movement again, this time with the hand turned over so that the palm of the hand is facing at least partly downwards. At once you will feel a tensing of the trapezius muscle behind your shoulder and the brachialis muscle between the upper arm

THE BACKSWING

and forearm, for these are the muscles that must now do the lifting.

Shoulders and hips

Golfers are often taught they must turn their shoulders by 90 degrees and their hips by 45 degrees in the backswing. Forget the angles. Just turn your hips and shoulders as far as you need to or as far as you can. Bobby Jones and Jack Nicklaus turned their bodies as far as they would go. Ben Hogan and Lee Trevino turned through a much smaller angle. All were great players with faultless backswings.

Another consideration in the backswing is the big quadriceps muscle in the front of the right thigh. The tendons of this powerful muscle are attached to the point of the hip. If you are seated as you read this, raise your leg off the floor a little and you will feel the quadriceps tense. If you create any tension in this muscle while balancing yourself, it will not be able to pull back your hip properly in the downswing, which shows again how critical posture and balance are to the golf swing. The front of the thigh must remain completely relaxed when you're balancing yourself, so that the nerve at the top of the muscle isn't triggered. One way to do this is to turn the right knee out a little more than the left. The muscle will then be able to elongate, allowing the knee to remain more or less where it is and the hip to turn freely to the right.

We saw before how essential it is to avoid swaying your right hip to the right as you raise the club. It is, of course, an extremely common fault. A sway to the right in the backswing always results in serious problems in the downswing, the technical reason being that it prevents you from positioning your left hip (which, of course, has been shifted to the right) above the left foot and so using the left hip efficiently as a pivot in the downswing. A simple remedy is to adopt the habit of moving your head to the right before the backswing. Once you have done this, it becomes difficult to sway your hip to the right, even if you want to.

Weight distribution

Probably the most harmful error golfers make here is to leave their weight on the left leg as they take the club back. Golfers who do this are a common sight—you see them with club aloft at the top of the backswing, still propped on a bent left knee. The fault lies in their failure to move their head to the right in the backswing. The backswing should end with the right ear over the right ankle and your weight over the right heel. The solution, therefore, is simply to turn your head and move it far enough to the right. It will then be physically impossible for you to remain stranded on your left leg.

At the other extreme, many golfers are obsessed by the idea that they have to deliberately transfer the weight of their body from one leg to another during the golf swing. This is one reason so many golfers sway their hips to the right. They feel a subconscious desire to get their weight *behind* the ball, in the mistaken belief that this will enable them to hit further. But the weight transfer exists mainly in their mind—it is largely an impression. Two things happen which create this impression. One is the simple shifting of the mass of the arms and the club (about 13 kilograms, or 28 pounds, on average) from one side of the body to the other. The other is the dynamic momentum of the arms and club as they move diagonally across the body at high speed, which produces the effect of weight.

Yet you still hear golf instructors speak of "the fundamentals of weight transfer". I have no doubt that "fundamentals" of this kind have ruined hundreds of thousands of golf swings over the years. The golfer has it fixed in his head that he has to transfer his weight to his right foot during the backswing. So he does it—and then wonders why he can't get the weight *off* his right leg when he swings the club down. To sum up: weight is transferred from one side of the body to another during the golf swing, but the transfer must not be a deliberate act. It is produced solely by the movement around the body of the weight of the arms and club.

The top of the backswing

At last, you have got the club fully raised. Where and how should the club be positioned now? The short answer is: "Anywhere and anyhow you like." We read in the textbooks that the club must be parallel with the ground and parallel with the target line at the top of the backswing. As if that's not hard enough, the left wrist must also be "square" and the face of the club must be square to the plane in which the club will swing down. All this is nonsense. I could name one hundred winners of majors who did not obey any of these rules. I could name another thousand golfers who did obey them—and did not win a tournament in their life.

Finish the backswing with the club in any position that suits you. Provided your hands are locked into position to drop into the slot and provided the muscles in your back are stretched and primed to pull the torso and arms back again, your backswing will be perfect.

THE DROP INTO THE SLOT

Having completed the backswing, the golfer must now drop his hands and arms into a position from which he can deliver the clubhead into the ball with maximum power. According to the laws of mechanics, the two arms and the club will deliver maximum power when as far as possible they are aligned in a single plane. Ben Hogan termed this common plane "the slot".

THE METHOD

There are three ways to ensure when you drop from the backswing plane into the downswing plane that you get into the slot. You can make sure the watch on your left hand is facing upwards ("Let God tell the time"); you can make sure the knuckles of your right hand are pointing downwards; or you can make sure that your right elbow drops down and under until it is pressed against your side. You will have time to think of only one of these, and it does not matter which one, for all three will get you into the slot. These are like three signposts that all point to the same destination.

Here, as always, having the right mental image of what you're trying to do can be enormously helpful. You may well find it easier to drop into the slot if mentally you can liken the movement you have to perform with the club to delivering a two-handed karate chop towards the inside of the ball. I suggest you put down this book, place the palms of your hands together and try this "karate chop" now, making sure that you aim the chop towards the side of the ball facing you. This effectively forces your right elbow into your side, where it needs to be.

THE MECHANICS

If you study a good golfer closely, you will see that the plane through which the club moves in the backswing is quite different from the plane of the downswing. After reaching the top of the backswing, the golfer

THE DROP INTO THE SLOT

needs to drop into the plane of the downswing before he can start swinging the club down. Many golfers aren't aware of this. They try to swing the club straight down from its final position at the top of the backswing, which is why so many of them hit from outside in. What they should be doing is moving their hands down from one plane to another, just as if they were moving from one floor of a building to another. This is what you do when you drop into the slot. You allow the weight of your two arms and the club to drop into that specific mechanical plane where the three levers work in unison.

If you study photographs of the top players, you find that they drop into this lower plane *before* the full rotation of the spine begins. In fact, this is obligatory, because they could not hope to drop into the lower plane after the spine had begun rotating back to the left. If the arms start to rotate before they are dropped downwards into the slot, the centrifugal force generated in the arms by this premature rotation is so great that it is impossible to then drop the arms correctly into place.

When you drop into the slot, you drop your right upper arm into your body and jam your right elbow against your side just above the hipbone. The elbow is then held in this position, virtually stationary, for most of the downswing, while the right forearm rotates around it. In other words, the right elbow is acting as a pivot for the forearm, which means that its precise positioning against your side is enormously important. A close study of the great players in action reveals that this positioning of the right elbow against the side is about the only thing in their golf swings that is the same. It does not matter how much their swings vary in other ways, all the great players from Norman back to Vardon have locked their right elbow at a point over or slightly to the front of the point of the hipbone. If the elbow is too far back, the hands will be moving too far to the inside by the time the clubhead reaches the ball, pulling the clubhead inside across the back of the ball. If the elbow is too far forward, the right hand will travel too wide too early, throwing the clubhead out across the target line.

Let's look once more at the mechanics of dropping into the slot. From the top of the downswing plane, your right upper arm drops down, pulling your right forearm down with it. It is when the right upper arm stops descending—that is, when the right elbow drops against your side—that the right forearm begins to rotate about the elbow in the downswing.

THE DROP INTO THE SLOT

This follows on from a correct backswing, shown overleaf.

In the downswing, the arms drop into the lower plane before the full rotation of the spine begins. By the time a golfer's hands are level with his belt, the upper body should still be largely closed to the target. The aim is to reach a position from which he can swing the arms and club through virtually a common plane.

THE BACKSWING
See pages 47-54

Note how the golfer's hands have begun to roll left palm down, right palm up. This position will be maintained as he continues through to the top of the backswing.

With the club shaft rising almost vertically from the hands, the effort required to lift the club into position at the top is minimized.

To get into the correct position at the top of the backswing, the golfer needs to move his head to the right and slightly backwards, so that the right ear ends up over the right ankle.

The golfer has moved his weight off the left foot to turn his body round the right hip.

IN THE SLOT

The golfer here, with her own individual style, has dropped her hands and the club shaft into the slot, a position from which she is able to swing her arms and the club through virtually a common plane.

THE DROP INTO THE SLOT

Once you have dropped your hands into the slot, the one thing to be on guard against is snapping your head back quickly towards the ball. If you allow your head to spin back like this too early, your shoulders will automatically spin back, too, and your golf swing will be in disarray. All the good work you did by getting into the slot will be spoiled. A sure way to prevent this happening is to continue facing towards the right for an instant after you have begun to rotate your body back towards the ball. Then, instead of pulling your shoulders around, your head will be pulled around by your shoulders.

The act of dropping your hands into the slot is accompanied by an interesting movement of your upper body to the left. It is interesting because until now this movement has passed virtually unnoticed, yet there can be no doubt that it takes place. You can confirm it by studying photographs of the top golfers in action and carefully measuring the positions of their various moving parts at different stages of the downswing. Until now, it has been thought that the hands moved away from the body as they dropped into the slot. In fact, the body moves away from the hands. What happens here is that the right side is shifting to the left in the downswing to allow the right elbow (which, of course, is locked against the right side) to move far enough to the left, towards the ball, to be in a position to act as a pivot for the right forearm.

All this enables us to finally understand the obscure function of those hip shifts and leftward leg actions that golfers perform in the downswing. Golfers have always liked to think that these play a positive role in the golf swing—that they somehow generate power. In fact, all that happens is that the hips move to the left to get the right elbow into the correct position relative to the ball, in the way I have just described. This movement of the hips is no more than a subconscious *reaction* to the needs of the right upper arm and elbow. Similarly, the movement of the legs to the left is just a subconscious *reaction* to the needs of the hips. I hope this lays to rest forever the myths about leg power and hip-shift power that so many golfers have believed in.

THE DOWNSWING

The downswing is the business end of the golf swing. Its purpose is to deliver the clubhead to the ball *from the right direction* so as to transmit to the ball as much as possible of the energy that has been concentrated in the slot. In other words, it's a continuation of the movement the golfer began when he dropped into the slot. For the downswing to be successful, you must hit downwards on the ball, which, of course, means that you must position yourself above, not behind, the ball. A successful downswing has one other key requirement: it must be a movement that the golfer can repeat regularly.

THE METHOD

Provided you have dropped your hands into the slot correctly, the downswing will proceed correctly, too, virtually of its own accord. There are just two things you need to worry about, and both concern the hands. The first is to keep your hands locked in the slot position—that is, with watch pointing up, right knuckles pointing down and right elbow firm against the side—for as long as possible. This will require a conscious effort, because what you are doing is overpowering the hands' natural inclination to roll over. Eventually, just before impact, the forces will become too great to resist, and at this point the hands will snap over and the arms will be pulled outwards.

Your other concern must be to ensure that the clubhead is delivered to the ball from the right direction. Most golfers wrongly think they have to deliver the clubhead into the back of the ball by swinging along the target line. But it is a mistake to see the golf swing as a movement forward towards the target—that is, from 6 o'clock on the ball to 12 o'clock. It is not. The force of the golf swing should be directed from 7 o'clock to 1 o'clock. The important thing here is your mental image of what you are doing. If you aim to hit the ball at 7 o'clock, the natural arc of the swing will ensure that the clubhead makes contact at the right angle. Although this may sound quite radical to many people

THE DOWNSWING

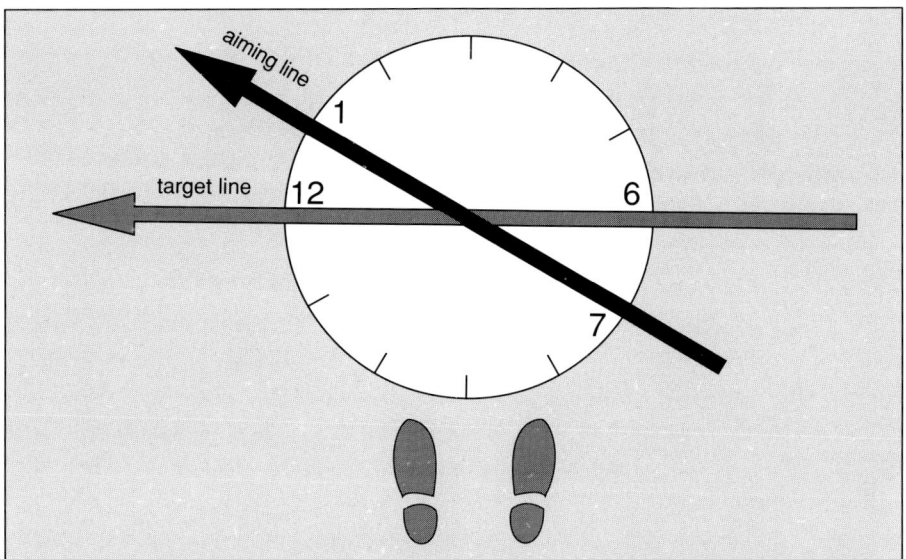

Hitting a golf ball presents a mental problem. The clubhead has to approach the ball from the inside, yet it must also hit the back of the ball. To the subconscious mind, the two things seem incompatible, which is why many golfers swing the clubhead out to try to approach the ball from behind —a fatal error. You can counter this with a mental image. Aim the clubhead at the inside of the ball— that is, think of hitting from 7 o'clock to 1 o'clock, not from 6 to 12—because this will force you to swing the clubhead in the correct path. In practice, your wrists will roll over at the last moment and you will actually hit the ball at 6 o'clock with a square clubface.

reading this book, it is a fundamental of correct technique. Think of hitting the ball sideways, not from behind. Think of aiming the heel of the club towards the inside of the ball instead of trying to throw the face of the clubhead towards the back of the ball. This particular mental imagery—that is, of aiming the butt of the club at the inside of the ball— makes the golfer keep his wrists cocked back, producing the late hit.

THE MECHANICS

Many golfers approach the golf swing with fear and suspicion. In fact, the golf swing is not unlike chopping wood with an axe. I have found this analogy extremely useful to older golfers and women especially. It is easy enough to imagine yourself chopping a log lying from side to side in front of you. Now, imagine the log was turned side on, so that you had to chop sideways into it. Again, this is a perfectly simple movement which you would have no trouble performing. You would turn your shoulders, turn the axe blade sideways and chop with much the same action as before. Well, the sideways chop with the axe actually has a lot in common with the downswing of the golf club. The fundamentals are the same.

The plane and direction of the downswing
The downswing is a roughly circular motion, powered by a rotation of the upper torso, and the plane it lies in is inclined somewhere between the plane of a ferris wheel and a merry-go-round. For this reason, the clubhead can never travel along the target line and into the back of the ball, as many golfers suppose it does. They are intent on getting their torso somehow *behind* the ball, so they face down the target line. Instead, they should be directing the force of the swing towards the *side* of the ball nearest to them. I call this playing golf sideways, and it is amazing how this different mental image of the swing can transform a golfer's game. If you concentrate on swinging the clubhead outwards in front of you into the side of the ball, instead of into the back of it, the shaft will do the rest for you. It will whip the clubhead around into the back of the ball, which explodes off the face of the club and flies like an arrow.

The start of the downswing
Jack Nicklaus has always insisted that he began the downswing while the clubhead was still on the way up, and if you watch a film of him in slow-motion, you will see this is true. There is no pause at all at the top of Nicklaus's swing. A fraction of a second before the clubhead reaches its high point, the lower half of Nicklaus's body is moving back in the direction of the ball. The lower half of his body is beginning the downswing while the upper half is still completing the upswing.

Most good golfers do this. It is, after all, the natural thing to do. Who ever saw a carpenter hammering a nail pause with the hammer in the air before bringing it down? Another reason is that the momentum of the clubhead still going back can act on your wrists to hold them in place. If the clubhead is still going back while the hands are starting to drop down into the slot, it will exert pressure on the wrists and so force your wrists to become cocked backwards, as they need to be in the slot.

The head
There are two controlling points in the downswing—your head and your hands—and virtually every fault you can make in the downswing can be traced to something you have done wrong with one of the two. Let us first consider the head. How often, after you have played a bad

THE DOWNSWING

shot, has one of your playing companions chided you by saying "You lifted your head"? The golfer who says this is right for the wrong reason. Your head may have been raised, but it isn't because you lifted it. Rather, it was an involuntary movement triggered by the body's automatic balancing mechanism. The lifting of the head is not the cause but the effect of some other fault. **Your head and your hips are counterbalanced.** If the hips move forward, your head will move upwards, whether you like it or not. It's only by keeping your hips behind your ankles that you will keep your head down. If you keep your hips back, your head will *have* to stay down.

Contrary to what you may have been taught, there is nothing wrong with turning the head in the downswing. In the backswing you should have turned your head to the right, and now you're turning it back again. But you must turn your head back *with* your shoulders, not before them. One of the worst things you can do in the entire golf swing is spin your head back towards the ball before you've got the rest of the downswing in motion, because the spinning of the head will cause the shoulders to spin, too. Then you will be in the position of having your head and shoulders turning ahead of your hips, which will spell disaster for your golf swing. The mistake many golfers make of shifting their weight onto their left foot too early is usually a result of spinning their head. As suggested before, a simple remedy is to keep looking to the right momentarily after your shoulders have begun to turn.

There is another head movement that causes problems early in the downswing—tilting the head to the left. By this I mean tilting it so that your left ear moves closer to your left shoulder. If this happens, you will automatically pull your left shoulder back and throw your right shoulder forward. If anything, tilt your head slightly to the right, because then you won't be able to spin your shoulders.

The hands

If you have read this far, you can be in no doubt that the hands are the primary means of control in the golf swing. In particular, it is by controlling the hands that you compel your arms and club to drop into the slot. I don't mean by this that the hands play any active or conscious part in directing the clubhead. They are rather like the captain who controls the ship from the bridge. He doesn't shovel coal or even turn dials—he just issues instructions to others down below, who obey them unquestioningly. If you make your hands move in a certain way, the rest

THE DOWNSWING

of the body will adjust itself in blind obedience to allow the movement to occur. The mere intention to use your hands in a certain way can trigger the rest of the body into action in the same way. This happens in the golf swing. What you intend to do with your hands dictates what the rest of the body does.

Now, dropping into the slot doesn't happen naturally. It is an acquired skill made possible by consciously controlling the way your hands move. To exercise this control, you must concentrate solely on the hands. If you try to think of what your hip is doing during the downswing, the hands will cease to be controlled and will revert to doing what comes naturally to them—that is, rolling over so that both thumbs are uppermost.

According to a theory that has been in vogue lately, the golfer should "take his hands out of the swing". The idea is that you let the big muscles control the swing. The opposite is true. How can you take your hands out of the swing when your entire body responds to what you intend to do with the hands? It is true, however that the hands cannot generate power in the downswing. Mechanically, the wrists act as free hinges, allowing angular momentum to accelerate the clubhead forward. Thus, the hands control the swing—but they do not power it.

Once you have got your hands into the slot in the correct position, the downswing will carry them on in this position automatically. All you have to do is resist the natural tendency of the hands to roll over. Everything will remain locked firmly in place as you swing your arms down. As part of this locking mechanism, the middle fingers of your right hand will be pulling back on the club while your left thumb will be pushing in the other direction. These opposing pressures (produced quite involuntarily) help to bind everything together.

As you begin the downswing with your hands locked in the slot position, aim to hit the ball at 7 o'clock, as I described before. To do this, you will need to change the mental image you have of the golf swing: it is a movement in the direction of 7 o'clock—not 6 o'clock.

Let us now take a broad look at what happens in the downswing. As we have seen, the butt of the club is subjected to two opposing pressures, one from the left thumb and the other from the middle fingers of your right hand. The hands remain locked in this position through the downswing, and the right elbow remains pressed against the side, and all the while the various forces are building. The centrifugal force of the club is trying to pull the right elbow away from the side, the left thumb is pushing against the middle fingers of the right hand, and the right hand is trying to do the natural thing and turn over. Finally, just before impact, the various forces become too great and the hands and arms, still locked in their unnatural position, break free, almost as if in an explosion. The right hand turns over, the right elbow pulls away from the side, the left wrist snaps straight, and the right arm is suddenly extended. The ball is then hit with maximum power.

Eliminating slack

If you have controlled your hands in the manner I set out before, the right arm should be forced automatically into the correct position—that is, bent at the elbow in a right angle, braced firmly against your right side and rotating in a radius. The importance of a firm right arm in this position is that it prevents slack from entering the swing. It is slack in the system that prevents you transmitting the power of the golf swing from its source (the turning of the torso) to its point of application (the clubhead). We may admire the golfer who has a loose, fluid, floppy swing, but this kind of golfer is rarely a power hitter, because there is too much slack in his system.

A good golf swing is something of much harder consistency than this. It is a welding together of many separate movements. Ben Hogan called it "being connected". Jack Nicklaus has called it "a solidness". In fact, all good golfers think of the golf swing in this way. The various parts of the swing are bonded together so firmly that there cannot be any slack. The power of the swing is transmitted through a solid system.

Golfers have always recognized the necessity of dropping the right elbow and bracing it against the side. Their mistake has been to try to do it deliberately. The result, invariably, is that they drop it too far. But if you have positioned your hands correctly, the elbow will drop against your side of its own accord.

The straight left arm

"Keep your left arm straight." This has always been regarded as a fundamental of golf, but it isn't. **A straight left arm doesn't make the golf swing correct.** Rather, a correct golf swing makes the left arm straight. If your swing is controlled properly by your hands, your left arm will straighten whether you like it or not.

The American golfer Ed Furgol was living proof of what I have been saying. His left arm was permanently bent, yet he won a US Open.

THE DOWNSWING

The black golfer Calvin Peete was another who had his left arm bent because of an injury, yet for a time he was the most consistent golfer on the American circuit. So far as the mechanics of the golf swing are concerned, the important thing is not having your left arm straight but making sure your left elbow does not bend and so allow slack to enter the system. Furgol and Peete had bent left arms, but they did not have flexible elbows. They simply positioned their spine to meet their own needs. During the backswing, as we saw earlier, you should pull your spine back from the ball a little so that your right ear can end up over your right ankle. Be sure to hold your spine back in the downswing, so that your torso and arms can be fully extended when you hit the ball.

The wide-arc theory
There are theorists who still promote this. The wider the arc of the swing, they say, the further you will hit the ball, so they advise golfers to move both arms as far to the right as possible at the start of the downswing. It is certainly true that when something rotates on a radius around a fixed point it will tend to move faster the further it is from this point of rotation. The wide-arc theorists seized on this basic law of physics, not realizing that although the law may work in a purely mechanical system such as a wagon wheel, it doesn't work in a flesh-and-bone system such as the human body which can be pushed and pulled about. If it did, we would all be using golf clubs 3 or 4 metres (10 or 12 feet) long. The wide-arc theory itself doesn't work, so forget it. If you try to adopt it, you will probably put yourself off balance and throw your right arm outwards. Then, the right arm will cease to be rigid, and slack will enter the system.

Having said that, I do concede that the wide-arc theory can benefit a golfer if it makes him move his spine further from the ball line. The need to extend the arms and shaft can sub-consciously make a golfer do this. But the wide-arc theory itself has no value whatever.

The hips and legs
Your hips and legs will do what they have to do automatically, provided your head and arms are moving correctly. If you spin your head too quickly, for instance, you will move onto your left leg too early. But the movement of the hips is not something you should think about consciously. If you do try to do so, you will lose control of the key element of the entire golf swing—the movement of the hands.

The point was made before that the legs do not generate any power in the golf swing. The idea that they do is based on a false sensation.

THE DOWNSWING
Eliminating slack

By forcing your hands down, you lock both shoulder joints into their sockets, eliminating any slack in the system.

By contrast, one can see that here the player's hands are already too high and too far from his torso. This will cause his shoulders to spin out, resulting in a weak, outside-in movement into the ball.

THE DOWNSWING

The movement of the hands

By holding your hands in the correct position, right palm up, left palm down, you force your arms into the correct position. This, in turn, brings the correct response from the rest of the body: the left hip clears, the left arm is extended and firm, and the right elbow locks inflexibly into position. You can simulate all these correct movements, without a club, by aiming a two-handed karate chop at the inside of the ball.

THE DOWNSWING

Because the movement of the legs and the slide of the hips during the golf swing *feel* so rapid and dramatic, golfers concluded they were somehow producing power. In fact, the reason for this rapid movement of the legs and hips is that the golfer's body is trying to get level with the ball so he can hit down on it. Jack Nicklaus is perfectly correct when he says that the further and faster he moves his legs and hips to the left, the further and straighter he hits the ball, but power in the legs and hips has nothing to do with this. The reason he hits further and straighter is simply that his legs and hips are bringing his body back into position faster to enable him to hit down on the ball.

Distribution of weight

A favourite topic of discussion among golfers is the supposed shift of weight from right foot to left foot during the downswing. Most golfers mistakenly believe it is body weight that is being shifted. If you examine the matter logically, you will see that this is impossible. It is accepted that the hips must not move from side to side in the golf swing—they should only rotate. But if your hips aren't moving sideways, what body weight is there to shift? The answer is that there is none.

The only weight transferred in the downswing is the weight of the arms and the club as they swing across the body. I cannot think of anything in golf so overlooked as the weight of the arms. In thirty years of researching human movement I have not known anyone in any sport to even admit the weight of the arms might be a factor. You hear the experts talking endlessly about "weight transfers" in golf and tennis and squash, but it never seems to occur to them that the arms have weight, too. In golf, there should be no deliberate relocation of body weight as such. It is the mechanical shifting of mass from one side of your body to another, plus the dynamic effect produced by the arms and club swinging down at high speed, that creates the sensation of weight moving from one leg to the other.

As the weight of your arms and the club moves across the body, you naturally move from the right foot to the left. One common mistake is to make this movement at the *start* of the downswing, before your torso has begun to turn. If you watch a good golfer closely, you will see that the transfer of "weight" from one foot to another is delayed until the very last moment—that is, until he is about to make contact with the ball. Take Greg Norman. He swings around on the right leg first, and it is only as his hands are dropping into impact that he shifts onto the left foot. He holds his "weight" on his right leg for so long that, once it has finally been shifted to the left, his right foot may be seen skidding across the grass towards his left heel. I must point out, however, that this isn't something Norman does deliberately. Like everything else in the downswing, it is a flow-on effect resulting from the way he controls his hands.

The slow swing

Of all the misconceptions about the golf swing, none is more widespread than the notion that the faster you swing the club, the further you hit the ball. In one sense, the exact opposite is true. The clubhead will move faster if you *slow* your hands—that is, if you pull back on the butt of the club and let the clubhead accelerate forward in a whiplash effect. This isn't something you have to make a conscious effort to do. The right hand will do it automatically if your hands are locked in the slot position and if the force of the swing is directed towards 7 o'clock on the ball.

It may be noted in passing that this pulling back by the right hand is beneficial for another reason. By putting extra pressure on the left thumb, it helps to lock the left arm rigid. The more you pull back with the right hand, the more solid and inflexible the left arm becomes. You can demonstrate this to yourself quite simply. Cock your left wrist back so that the thumb is extended at right angles to the forearm, and then push the thumb against the two middle fingers of your right hand—the two fingers, remember, that really hold the club. This roughly simulates what happens in the downswing. The harder the left thumb pushes forward and the harder the two fingers of the right hand pull it back, the more securely the left arm is locked into position. This is why golfers such as Ben Hogan and Byron Nelson were seen to have such rigid left arms at the moment of impact.

The famous pro Henry Cotton devised an unusual training exercise which by all accounts produced marvellous results. He got his pupils to hold a club in their right hand and bang it repeatedly against a car tyre, the idea being that this would strengthen their wrist. I would argue that the reason this exercise was successful has nothing to do with the strength of the wrist. Rather, it was because the exercise taught people how to put a brake on the butt of the club with the middle fingers of their right hand. To hit the tyre with the club, they had to stop the butt of the club, which is precisely what the golfer must do in the golf swing. Cotton's training exercise did help his pupils, but not for the reason he thought it did.

THE DOWNSWING

The slow turn

As he rotates in the downswing with his arms swinging outwards, the golfer is like a turning maypole in a children's playground. We all know that when a maypole is turned, the chains attached to the top of it begin to fly out. The faster the pole is turned, the higher the chains fly. It is the same with the golfer. The faster he turns in the downswing, the more his arms and the club will be pulled outwards by centrifugal force, causing the golfer to swing the clubhead outside the line and so hit from outside in. Turning too fast has another serious consequence. Because more centrifugal force is generated, the weight of the arms pulls the golfer forwards and off balance. To counteract this, the body's automatic balancing mechanism causes the golfer to pull his upper body back and lift his head. Now, lifting the head is accepted as being one of the most common faults in golf, yet very few people understand what causes golfers to do it. In fact, it is an involuntary response to maintain balance, and the golfer is powerless to resist it. The solution is to slow the rotation of the torso, so that your balance is not in danger. You can do this by keeping your right elbow firmly against your side. Keeping your right elbow there makes it anatomically difficult for the torso to spin quickly—a fact you can demonstrate to yourself by standing up and rotating your torso, first with the right arm extended and then with the elbow pressed against the side. The difference will be obvious.

The late hit

The ideal downswing has the clubhead accelerating in the final instant to achieve maximum velocity—the "late hit" that good golfers speak about. The point was made before that, despite countless claims to the contrary, this cannot be achieved by a deliberate movement of the hands at the last moment. The downswing is too rapid a movement to allow refinements of this kind to be made deliberately. Rather, the last-minute acceleration occurs quite naturally, provided everything else in the downswing is correct.

The laws of physics are on the golfer's side here. As you swing out and downwards, the clubhead develops centrifugal force—that is, a force that tends to make it fly off at a tangent—and this build-up of centrifugal force pulls at the arms and has the effect of slowing them down. The same law of physics is used by ballerinas doing pirouettes. If a ballerina extends her arms outwards, she slows down. If she folds them into herself, she speeds up.

Now, because your hands are slowing down, the clubhead has time to catch up in a final whiplash-type movement which brings the shaft into line with your arms just at the instant you make contact with the ball. This explains why many leading golfers deliberately slow the start of the downswing when they want to hit further. Sam Snead and Jack Nicklaus are two who have made a point of this. As we saw, if the club is accelerated early in the downswing, centrifugal pull will develop too quickly and will overpower the momentum of the shaft and so drag on the hands. In effect, the club becomes too heavy too soon. To prevent this, start turning your torso more slowly and so bring the clubhead down more slowly at first. The more slowly you start the clubhead down, the longer it will take for the centrifugal force to build up.

The longer you can delay the release of the wrists in the downswing, the greater will be the whiplash effect just before impact, which is what really gives the swing its power. One way to delay this release is to have a mental image of aiming the butt of the club at the inside of the ball as you swing the club down. As well as automatically forcing your right elbow against your side, where it needs to be, this will ensure that your wrists remained cocked for as long as possible.

Timing the ball is either something you will do quite naturally, without giving it a thought, or something you will learn from experience. I've known many golfers who had trouble mastering the knack of timing, and my advice to them has been to practise with an extra-long shaft. If they normally use a standard (43 1/2 inch) shaft, they should trying swinging with a shaft 2 or 3 inches (5 to 8 centimetres) longer. When you use a long shaft, the sensation produced by the growing centrifugal force is exaggerated, and because you can feel the force more easily you will be better able to control it. This is why some fishermen use a very long rod when they are trying to acquire the knack of casting a line. The length of the rod forces them to swing it more slowly, and by doing so they can feel the various forces coming into play and so learn to co-ordinate them.

The clubhead on impact

The thing to recognize here is that the clubhead is rotating at the end of a radius and is therefore moving through an arc, not along a straight line. It can only hit the ball at a point in its arc. It cannot, as many golfers like to think, approach the ball in a straight line. (Because of an interplay of various forces, it can happen that the clubhead will approach the ball along the target line for a few centimetres [an inch or so], but this is not

THE DOWNSWING

something you can control). The clubhead certainly cannot approach the ball along the target line for any measurable distance. It must approach it in an arc from inside the target line (which is the right thing to do) or from outside (which is wrong). At the same time, it is obvious that the clubhead must be delivered into the back of the ball. Now, the need to do these two things creates a problem in the minds of many golfers, for somehow they seem contradictory. The golfer feels instinctively that if he brings the club down from the inside, as he is required to do, he will hit the side of the ball instead of the back of the ball. Instead of hitting the ball at 6 o'clock towards 12 o'clock, he will hit it at 7 o'clock towards 1 o'clock.

My solution is to counter one mental image with another. I tell golfers who have this problem to try *deliberately* to hit the ball at 7 o'clock towards 1 o'clock (see the diagram on page 59). When they try to hit it at 7 o'clock, they actually succeed in hitting it at 6 o'clock, the reason being that the mental image of what they are trying to do is compatible with the direction from which they are swinging the club. I have never known this mental trick to fail to work.

The angle of the clubface as it strikes the ball should be of secondary importance in the learning process. The first thing to do is to get your golf swing operating properly, so that the clubhead is repeatedly being delivered to the ball from the right direction. Only then should you worry about the angle of the clubface. Many golfers put the cart before the horse. They concentrate so hard on trying to get the clubface square at impact that they roll the clubface over at the start of the downswing.

It is worth noting that ideally the clubhead makes contact with the ball not at the bottom of its arc but fractionally before it. The clubhead is still heading downwards at the moment of impact, although the loft of the clubface compensates for this. Many inexperienced golfers try to hit under the ball, believing that this will help them get the ball in the air, and as a result they hit the turf first and the ball second. Trying to hit under the ball invariably makes your right shoulder drop and your left shoulder rise, thus depriving the golf swing of power.

Instead, you ought to be hitting slightly *down* on the ball—that is, hitting the ball first and the turf second. The divot you make should be a few centimetres (about an inch) in front of where the ball was, not behind it. The same thing is true when you're hitting off the tee. If you watch the tournament golfers, you will see that they all hit *down* with the

THE DOWNSWING

driver, just as they do with an iron, even if most of them think they are actually hitting up into it. If you study photographs of the really long hitters, you will notice something else: although they are hitting slightly downwards, they do hit the bottom half of the ball. They thus hit the ball high on the clubface of the driver, not in the middle of it, and impart a spin on the ball which holds it in the air much longer.

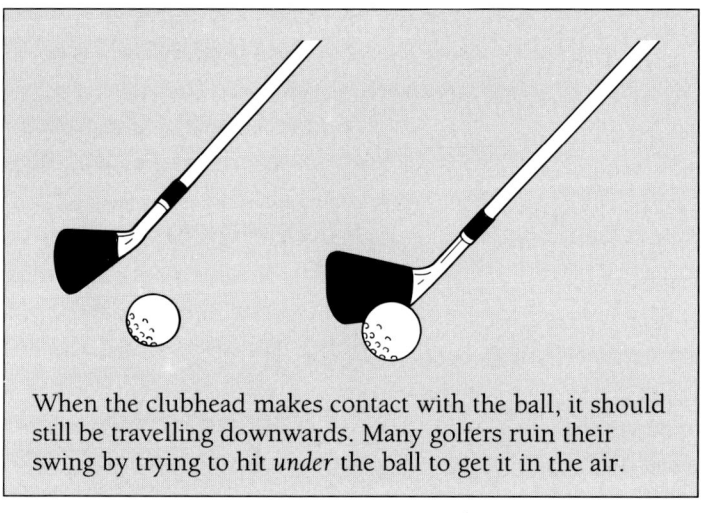

When the clubhead makes contact with the ball, it should still be travelling downwards. Many golfers ruin their swing by trying to hit *under* the ball to get it in the air.

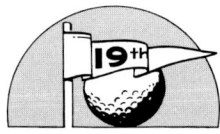

THE
FOLLOW-THROUGH

The chapter I devote to the follow-through must necessarily be short, for there is almost nothing constructive you can say on the subject. Some authorities claim that the follow-through is an integral part of the golf swing. Their argument is that by concentrating on how you intend to follow through, you can influence the way you hit the ball. This is true. **Concentrating on the follow-through will certainly influence how you hit the ball. But the influence will be destructive.**

The brain, as we have seen, is able to pre-program almost any movement you would like to perform. If you ask your brain to pre-program a high, flowing follow-through which ends with your hands over your head, you will certainly get what you want. Whether you also manage to hit the ball is another matter. By concerning yourself with the follow-through, you are sure to turn your head and ruin your swing. So forget about the follow-through entirely. Let the follow-through take care of itself when the time comes—as undoubtedly it will if your golf swing up to that point is correct.

I go further and advise ordinary golfers not to think of hitting *through* the ball, as the textbooks suggest, but rather *to* the ball. Again, it is a question of having the right mental image. If you concentrate on hitting *to* the ball, you will be inclined to slow your hands before you make impact, because subconsciously you will be looking upon the moment of impact as the end of the golf swing. As we have seen, slowing the hands makes the clubhead accelerate faster and enables you to hit with greater power.

IN THE BUNKER

There is a fundamental flaw in the way most golfers try to play bunker shots. I'm not speaking here only of weekend golfers. Even in the professional ranks there are very few golfers you could honestly describe as outstanding sand players. The problem golfers encounter in the bunker is common to all. They feel subconsciously that they have to make a tremendous effort to drive the club through the sand, so they tend to smash at the ball with the right arm. What happens when they do this is that the right hand rolls over the left too early and by too much, causing the blade of the club to turn and point left as it enters the sand. As a result, the clubhead is slowed more than it should be. It also loses much of its loft and, therefore, much of its capacity for imparting spin to the ball.

To play a controlled bunker shot and get enough spin on the ball, it is absolutely essential that you don't permit the slightest closure of the clubface as you drive the club into the sand. When the clubface is closed, it picks up a huge amount of sand, which, as I said before, tends to slow it down.

I can offer a foolproof method of ensuring that your right hand doesn't roll over and close the clubface. What you must do is change the direction of the downswing. Begin by standing open to the target line and taking the club back as you normally would. Now, instead of swinging your hands down in the ordinary way, aim to pull your right hand across your left toe as you hit the ball. In this way, your right hand is forced to stay behind your left hand. This not only prevents the clubface closing, it actually opens it slightly, which enables you to put more spin on the ball.

I am not suggesting, of course, that you pull the clubhead itself towards your left foot. Obviously, it must travel towards the ball. It is only the hands that are pulled to the left and turned so that the right hand moves inside. But when the hands are turned, they also turn the clubhead.

THE FOLLOW-THROUGH

If you have swung the club correctly, the follow-through will take care of itself. Note how the golfer's entire upper body has followed the club as far as his left foot and leg will allow him to.

THE SWEET SPOT
See page 70

If your swing is good, the ball will always hit the "sweet spot", which is above the bottom of the clubface.

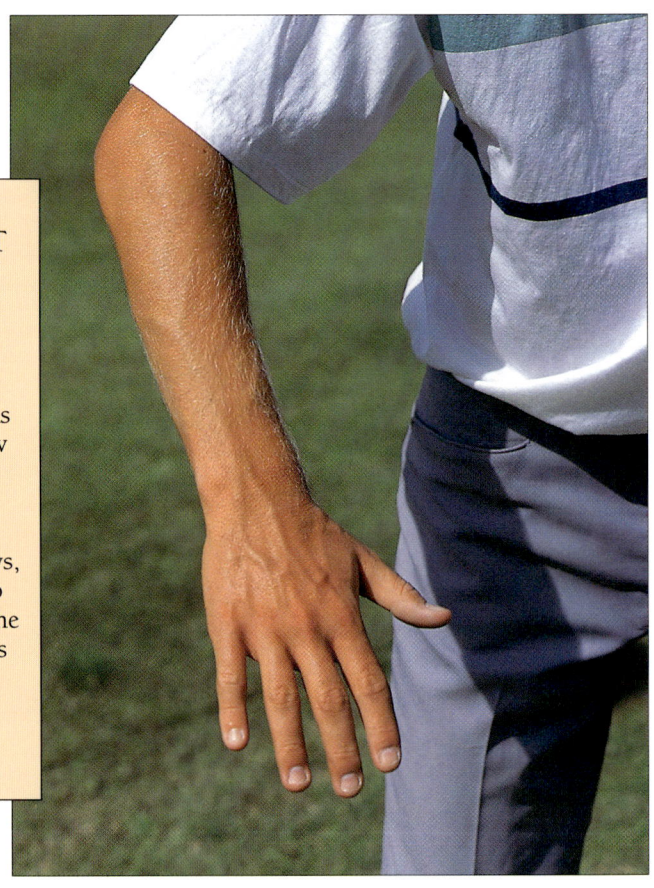

THE CLUBHEAD ON IMPACT
See page 69

If you try to get the clubface square from the top of the backswing, the tendency is to roll the right hand too soon. As a consequence, the right elbow is pulled out and away from the body, resulting in a weak, outside-in pass at the ball. As the photograph opposite shows, this also forces the right hip to move to the right, back over the right foot. This, in turn, causes the left leg to straighten and stiffen, preventing the lower body weight from shifting to the left, as it should.

IN THE BUNKER

When too much sand is built up between the ball and the clubface, like earth built up on the blade of a bulldozer, the energy of the clubhead cannot be transmitted to the ball.

The golfer's hands are coming down very steeply to the ball from the open-stance position.

The hands have continued across the body, passing over the left toe.

IN THE BUNKER

The other advantage to be gained from this technique is that you slice into the sand with the narrow sole of the clubhead rather than slap it with the flat face, so the sand doesn't offer nearly so much resistance. You can tell at once from the noise whether you have done this correctly. The noise the sole of the club makes when it hits the sand is very distinctive and could never be confused with the thud of the closed blade.

All this enables you to give the ball more spin and more height, and, most important of all, you will never find the ball still sitting in the sand after you hit at it. Remember not to drive the club too deep into the sand. That, too, can kill the spin. You need to scoop into the sand just far enough behind the ball to get the blade under the ball.

The impulse to smash the head of the sandiron into the sand, which I referred to before, causes golfers to swing their hands and arms too fast and too far, with the result that their hands are well in front of the blade as it enters the sand. If you examine a sandiron at different angles to the ground, you will see that the further the butt of the club is ahead of the clubhead, the less effective loft there is on the blade and the greater the area of clubface that has to be dragged through the sand. Conversely, the more upright the shaft is, the greater the loft and the smaller the area of clubface to be forced through the sand. This urge to smash at the sand is part of an image problem. The ordinary golfer feels he has to pick up a huge load of sand with the clubface and somehow lift the sand and the ball onto the green.

Most textbooks advocate, correctly, that in the bunker the clubhead should be raised and then brought down at as steep an angle as possible, because this ensures that there is a minimum of clubface forced through the sand. To help golfers appreciate what needs to be done here, I sometimes suggest a simple exercise. From a position of address, I tell them simply to turn the club upside down, so that the butt points at the ground, and then drop it back to its ordinary position. The purpose is to enable golfers to experience the steepness of the movements that are required. The downswing is not a pulling along of the ball but, rather, a positive driving movement almost straight down and then along.

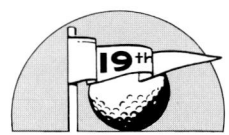

PUTTING
NATURAL IS BEST

When a golfer goes to the pro for a lesson on putting, he is really asking to be turned into a kind of geometrical robot. He wants the pro to tell him how to get everything square, everything measured up and lined up, and how to manoeuvre the putter through and along the geometrical lines thus created. If that golfer came to me instead, I would use a different approach. I would put six balls on the green and, without specifying a target, ask him to hit them. If they all went roughly the same distance and in roughly the same direction, I would say to him, "I've just taught you to putt."

The simplest and best way to putt is to do whatever comes most naturally to you. Once you have established what your natural putting action is, then by all means make minor adjustments to it. (I will describe later how this can be done.) The key to successful putting is being able to trust the putter to do the same thing every time—and the more natural the movement, the easier it is to repeat.

I continue to be amazed by the complexities of technique that have been introduced into putting. Take the grip. Golfers are told they must have this finger running along behind that one, which in turn is overlapped by the one that is sticking out from under some other finger. **It is not surprising that golfers often end up with a grip that looks more like a pound of sausages in a plastic bag than anything else.** Ignore all this kind of nonsense. Simply grip the putter in a way that feels natural and comfortable and hit the ball. My only advice on holding the putter is this: grip the shaft firmly with the two middle fingers of the right hand, because this will tend to lock the wrist. What you must try not to do is to allow the right wrist to swing freely. Also, try to have all the fingers exerting more or less the same pressure on the club. Many golfers, without realizing it, grip the club tightly with the index finger of their right hand while allowing the middle fingers to relax, as a result of which the wrist breaks and turns over.

If the ball tends to go to the left of the target, don't change your grip or your putting action. Simply close your shoulders a fraction so they are pointing slightly further to the right. This will make the ball go straight. By rotating the upper body in this way in either direction, it is possible to adjust your putting line while still keeping your natural grip and putting action intact. I call this "dialling a putt".

One of the worst pieces of advice you can give a golfer is to tell him he must remain perfectly still while he putts. The golfer has enough to think about on the putting green without having to concentrate on whether he might be moving a knee or a shoulder. It is also wrong to tell him to begin moving the putter slowly and then accelerate it. In fact, the opposite is correct—the earlier you accelerate the club, the better.

The most common mistake golfers make when they go to putt a ball is to concentrate on the backswing. They force their brain to focus on it as if it were the secret to putting success. Now, the brain can do many astonishing things, but it cannot pre-program reverse movements. It cannot come up with a single program in advance for two movements in opposite directions, even if one follows the other immediately. The best the brain can do is program them separately, as though they were independent of each other, which means that what you do in the backswing cannot improve the way you perform the only swing that matters—the putt for the hole.

So, forget the backswing. Concentrate on hitting the ball where you intend it to go, and you will probably find it goes there. Take the putter back briskly and then start moving the hands forward before the head of the putter has gone all the way back. The worst thing you can do with a putter is to slow down your natural movement with a cautious and deliberate backswing, because what this does is to bring muscles of opposition into play, which are likely to produce a jerk reflex. This kind of jerk is typical of a player with the yips.

If you're hammering a nail, you don't worry about how you're lifting the hammer. You think only of how you're hitting the nail, so you don't even pause at the top of the upswing. The head of the hammer is still going up when the hand holding the hammer has started to come down. It's much more natural to use your putter in the same way, so that the end of the backswing merges into the start of the forward swing.

The preoccupation that golfers have with symmetrics is nowhere more obvious than on the putting green. Golfers mesmerize themselves with symmetrics as soon as they pick up a putter. That has to be square with this, and this has to be parallel with that. Probably the best putter the game has known, Bobby Locke of South Africa, had nothing square or parallel. His feet were this way, his shoulders that way. He rolled his hips and shifted his knees. But he had found a way of putting that suited him, he had practised it, and he came to trust it entirely.

It's actually much easier to be non-symmetrical than it is to be symmetrical. It's much easier to let the face of the putter open or close when you take the putter back than it is to keep it dead square, as most golfers try to do. Billy Casper hooded the putter, as did Bobby Locke. Casper allowed the putter blade to swing upwards and then downwards through the natural arc of a true pendulum. Bobby Locke, on the other hand, hooded the blade and then deliberately pulled it to the inside, thus forcing himself to move the putter head around himself and through the ball to impart "hookspin" to the ball. In other words, like everything else in the golf swing, putting is action and reaction.

What Casper and Locke did was the natural thing for them. But if you prefer to open the face of the putter as you bring it back, then it is more natural to keep it low to the ground, with a sweeping motion. So the choice is up to you—hood the putter or open it—but once you've made the choice, do the natural thing. Don't mismatch it with another movement that is incompatible. If you hood the putter, raise it in the air. If you open it, keep it low to the ground (see photographs between pages 80 and 81).

The principal rule of putting is: if it needs to move, let it move—Bobby Locke moved everything, and he was the best.

PUTTING—A MIND TEST

More than anything else, putting is a test of mental strength. That four-and-a-quarter-inch hole in the ground you have to aim for is one of the most negative things I know of in sport. If you stood a four-and-a-quarter-inch jam tin on the green and asked the average golfer to putt the ball from a metre (3 feet) away and hit it, he would probably succeed nine times in ten. When he has to drop the ball into a hole instead, he might be lucky to do it five times in ten. The hole itself creates a mental block. The secret is just to think about where the ball is starting from: if you start it right, it will finish right.

There are other kinds of mental blocks in putting. One is a visual one. If you line up a putt with the putter resting behind the ball, as most golfers do, the conflict between the shapes of the round ball and the flat putter head tend to create a visual confusion which makes it difficult for you to assess clearly how the ball needs to be hit. Many golfers have been conscious of this problem, even if they had no idea what was causing it, and a few have hit upon a solution. Instead of lining up the putt with the putter behind the ball, they move the putter head towards them, so that the toe of the putter is just *inside* the ball.

In this way, they get a clear view of how the clubface is lying relative to the target and an unobstructed visual image of the putt they have to make. They begin the backswing with the putter in this position but, of course, bring the putter head down the target line in the forward swing. Bobby Jones and Bobby Locke, two great putters, both used this method. Greg Norman did, too, and for a time he was the best putter on the circuit. Then he abandoned it, and he has not been the same putter since.

You can create another kind of mental block for yourself by staring at the ball. My cure is to place a five-cent coin just inside the ball and to tell golfers to look at the coin and nowhere else while they're lining up the putt. The cure is usually instantaneous. Once they cease to be mesmerized by the ball and putter head, they immediately revert to playing a smooth, easy putting stroke.

The yips have other causes, too, of course. There is one that even the experts don't seem to be aware of—allowing your chin to sink towards your chest. When your chin drops like this, it engages muscles right down the front of your torso and the front of your legs, which makes it virtually impossible to move your shoulders and arms without moving your head. To avoid this, go down over the putter with your chin well clear of your chest. Then, you will be supported entirely by the muscles in your back, and the muscles in the front of your torso will be completely relaxed.

I have found it helps some golfers to think of putting in terms of *rolling* the ball. To reinforce this mental image, I suggest to them that they should aim to hit the top of the ball—that is, to roll it along rather than hit it. What this does is make the golfer hit slightly upwards, which in turn stops his hands moving and allows the head of the putter to move ahead of his hands. This counters a tendency of many golfers to let their hands move ahead of the putter head, a cause of numerous problems.

MORE ABOUT TURNING

In an earlier chapter we examined the essential features of the backswing. I suggest we now reflect on the whole question of why and how the shoulders and hips need to be turned. I do so for the benefit of those who seek a deeper understanding of the mechanics of turning, a subject that over the years has been largely misunderstood. If you know *why* you turn and *what* you turn, if you've got a true mental image of what you're trying to do, you will naturally do it better.

Let us return to the start of the backswing. The immediate question is how the golfer should initiate the backswing. In other words, what primary movement should he concentrate his mind on to get the backswing under way? There are many schools of thought here. A generation ago, many golfers believed that taking the club back ought to be the primary movement. The movement of the arms, they said, caused the shoulders and then the hips to turn, all of which had the effect of winding up the body like a spring. In recent years, many golfers (including top players such as Greg Norman and Tom Watson) have argued that the primary movement should be pulling back the right hip—or, as it is often expressed, pulling back the hip pocket. There are other variations. For instance, Jack Nicklaus's dominant thought as he began the backswing was "to load the right heel very early"—an interesting concept which I will deal with later. What we need to do is isolate what turns first and why.

I suggest we go back one step further and examine precisely which parts of our body we ought to be turning. The spine is obviously one of them, but bear in mind that the spine isn't like a length of rubber that can be twisted endlessly. It's a chain of solid segments, the vertebrae, each of which is capable of only a very limited movement. A rotation of the spine is really a spiral twist—an accumulation of the small movements made by the many individual vertebrae. In fact, the average spine can be twisted by only 30 degrees, and if you add this to the recommended turn of the hips, 45 degrees, you have a total turn of about 75 degrees. Yet

MORE ABOUT TURNING

golfers are told they ought to be turning their shoulders by as much as 90 degrees in the backswing. Where do we find the other 15 degrees?

The answer to this previously neglected question is critical to an understanding of the backswing turn. Contrary to the popular view, the shoulders aren't a solid entity like a coathanger. The bones of the upper arms are attached quite loosely to the torso, and each is capable of wide-ranging and independent movement, both forwards and back. It is precisely this kind of movement that people make when they "pull their shoulders back" or "hunch their shoulders forwards". It is the tops of their arms they are moving here, not their shoulders as a single unit. This is where those other 15 degrees come from. As well as turning his hips and his spine, the good golfer pulls the top of his left arm forwards around his chest and the top of his right arm behind his back, producing a total, visible turn of the "shoulders" of about 90 degrees when added to the turning of the hips and spine. This may all seem self-evident when you think about it, yet it is an area where the average golfer often loses out. He tries to turn only the spine, without moving the tops of his arms, and then he wonders why he can't achieve a nice, full, backswing turn. Moving the tops of your arms doesn't come naturally. You have to practise it and build it into your swing.

Here is an important point to keep in mind which may save you back problems in the future: it is not essential to turn your spine as far as it will go. On the contrary, to do so is wrong for two reasons. First, the further you turn the spine, the more you risk damaging your vertebrae and discs. Second, the further you rotate the spine in one direction, the more you set up an instantaneous, reflex spinning of the torso in the other direction. The importance of this is that the faster and further you spin your torso in the downswing, the more your arms will be pulled outwards by centrifugal force and the more you will throw the clubhead outwards across the ball.

A remark by Ben Hogan many years ago provided me with a vital insight into the movement of the shoulders in the backswing. Hogan happened to mention that he always wore out a patch just inside the left shoulder of his golf shirt, where it came into contact with his chin at the top of his backswing. To appreciate the significance of this, you must first recognize the largely unrecognized fact that as well as being able to move *around* the upper torso, as described before, the top of a golfer's arm can also move *upwards* relative to the torso, towards his ear. Again,

MORE ABOUT TURNING

this is not a movement of the shoulders as such, but an independent movement of the top of the arm. Clearly, the tip of Hogan's left shoulder must have made such a movement when he raised the club. Indeed, to come in contact with his chin, it must have made a huge movement to the left, which meant that he did not need to twist his spine so far.

Here the plot thickens. It is a fact that the huge trapezius muscles above and behind each shoulder (see the diagram overleaf) operate as opposites to the big frontal and back chest muscles that are attached to the tops of the arms. If the trapezius is tensed up and active, the others will be relaxed and inactive, and vice versa. Try this experiment. Stand up and extend a rigidly straight left arm in front of you, with the fist firmly closed, as if you were addressing the ball. If you feel the muscles in front of the left shoulder with your right hand, you will feel that they are firm and tense. By locking your left elbow, you have effectively locked the top of your left arm to your chest and so severely restricted its ability to move around freely in front of your chest. This shows us at once how absurd it is to lock your left arm straight when you address the ball, as some textbooks have advocated. It also explains why many top players over the years have advocated letting the arms hang in a relaxed fashion from the shoulders when addressing the ball.

Since the right, or dominant, arm and hand will receive more of your conscious attention during both the backswing and downswing, it obviously makes more sense, when you address the ball, to accommodate the right arm and hand first and then, and only then, fit a slightly bent and relaxed left arm into the available space. (This conflicts entirely with the accepted theory that you must set the straight left arm first and then reach down and under the left hand to place your right hand on the grip.) To give your left arm more room, it clearly makes sense to raise the tip of your left shoulder towards your ear, as Hogan did. You are now in an ideal position. Your spine is not bowed, your right arm and hand are perfectly positioned, and by engaging the trapezius to raise your left shoulder you have relaxed the chest muscles which previously had been bound up like a chicken ready for the oven. Don't overdo it. Don't lift the tip of your left shoulder right up to your ear. Just raise it enough so that it can sweep around freely at roughly the level of your chin.

Conversely, if you push the tip of your left shoulder downwards and/or engage those big frontal and back muscles, your spine will bow. Viewed from the back, it will be curved like the parenthesis symbol:).

PUTTING
See pages 74-77

The sequences on this page and overleaf clearly show the player taking the heel of the putter back first—a movement known as hooding the putter face. This movement sets up a one-piece pendulum movement of the shoulders, arms and putter back and through the ball.

The putting action requires no power: it is a caress rather than a hit, performed by very soft hands.

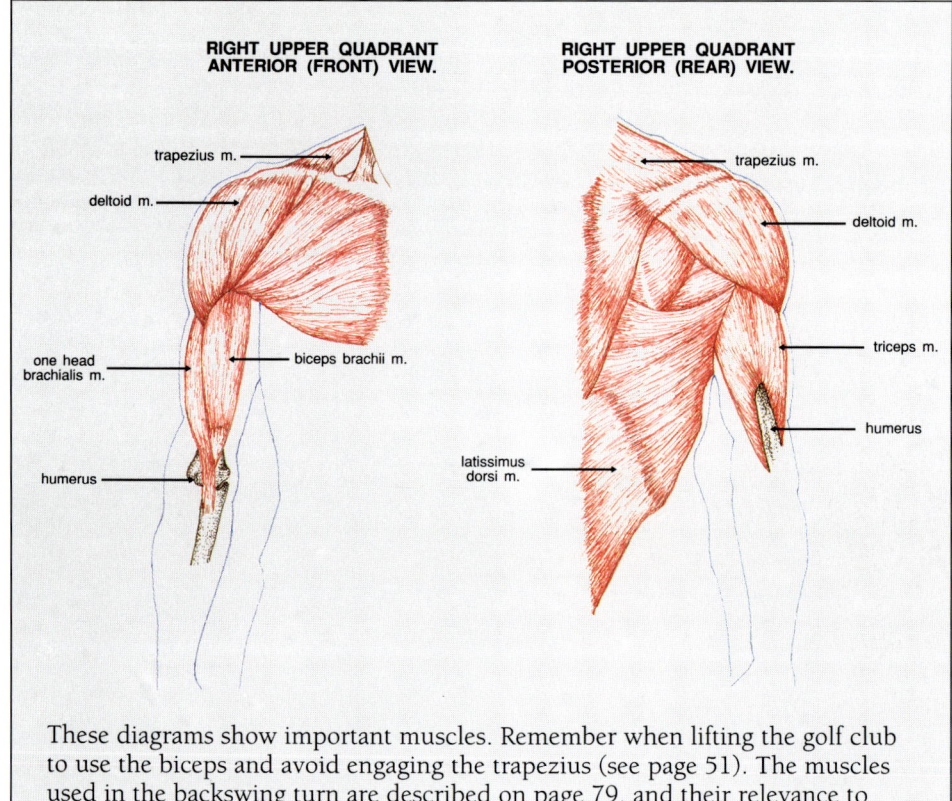

These diagrams show important muscles. Remember when lifting the golf club to use the biceps and avoid engaging the trapezius (see page 51). The muscles used in the backswing turn are described on page 79, and their relevance to putting is mentioned on page 80.

MORE ABOUT TURNING

This will result in your hips being pushed over the right foot, which is where they will remain for the rest of the golf swing. But if you *raise* the tip of your left shoulder when you address the ball, as I recommend, your hips will move a little towards your left heel, which is precisely where they ought to move in preparation for the downswing.

I referred before to Jack Nicklaus's statement that his prime mental trigger for the backswing was "to load the right heel". This, I suggest, is a case of the brain getting the body to react to what we intend to do. Nicklaus's intention was to *feel* the weight of his upper body masses over his right heel—not to deliberately move those masses there. His brain would register the intention, organize the necessary movement of the upper body, and so give Nicklaus what he asked for—that is, the feeling of having his weight over his right heel at the top of the backswing. In fact, all the great players move their weight dramatically towards their right heel during their backswing, so much so that they can raise the toes of their right foot off the ground. Knowing this, you should now consciously try to do what they do subconsciously. To do it, you must breach one of golf's so-called fundamentals and move your head towards your right heel. As you do so, you must also move your coccyx bone a little to the left—a point I will look at more closely later.

Here is another intriguing fact which, so far as I know, has never been commented on: **a golfer's torso is further from the ball at impact than when he addresses the ball.** This really ought to be obvious. When a golfer addresses the ball, there is always a pronounced angle between the club shaft and his extended arms. At impact, the club shaft and his arms are much closer to being in a straight line, which means his torso must be further from the ball, which, after all, is a fixed object. This is consistent with the fact that he has moved his weight towards his right heel during the backswing. Thus, the two things come together. I spoke before of backswing "triggers". I suggest that the best trigger for your backswing is a conscious movement of your right ear diagonally towards your right ankle, accomplished by moving your body (including the spine) as a single unit. As simple as that!

I may add here that the critical thing in this manoeuvre is not so much moving your weight but moving your *spine* back towards your right heel and holding it there in the downswing to allow the added extension of the arms.

Let's now study the hips. Elsewhere in this book I make the point that during the backswing and the early part of the downswing the golfer must pivot on his right leg. Through impact and beyond he must pivot on his left leg. Now, the legs don't merely shift and support body weight. They must also provide a brace to resist the centrifugal forces that are tending to pull the golfer forwards during the downswing. To achieve this bracing effect, the right leg must be positioned to do it beforehand, and since you must pivot about your right leg and right hip joint for most of the working part of the golf swing, it makes sense to position that leg first. Mechanically, this is accomplished by moving the weight of the upper body towards and over the right heel. By doing so, it is obvious that the right hip joint must move back a little from its position when you addressed the ball.

This turning of the hips is not a single event but the product of a sequence of events. What starts the sequence off? One way to investigate this is to study photographs of the great players taken from the back. What you must do here is fix upon some part of the hips as a reference point, such as the coccyx bone at the bottom of the spine. If you trace the movement of a player's coccyx during the backswing, you will find that it moves some distance to the *left* of where it was when he was addressing the ball. You will also find that at the top of the backswing his right upper leg is pointing downwards well to the right of his right heel. Since the bone of the upper leg is the primary line of force for the weight borne by that leg, this means that his weight at the top of the backswing must be very much on the *outside* of his right heel. This disposes of another time-honoured "fundamental" of golf technique— namely, that the right leg must be braced so that the knee points inwards and that the weight must remain on the inside of the right foot during the backswing. Whatever they may say to the contrary in their textbooks, all top golfers splay their knees. Indeed, they position their upper legs at much the same angle as used in an A-frame— at about 75 degrees.

The photographic evidence, on top of the other facts I have adduced, makes it clear that not only does the right hip joint move slightly back during the backswing but the hips themselves move to the left. In fact, at the top of a mechanically perfect backswing the hips will be as far to the left as they will be at impact. What precisely do the hips do during the downswing? The top golfers have given us conflicting accounts of this, based on what what they *felt* their own hips were doing.

What happens is mechanically quite simple. During the backswing,

MORE ABOUT TURNING

the right hip joint, acting as a mechanical pivot with the firmed right leg as a brace, moves through a shallow arc backwards and towards the left foot. This initiates a reaction on the opposite side of the body, which starts the sequence. First, the left hip joint responds by moving through a shallow arc slightly forwards and towards the right foot. It is important to recognize here that the right hip joint, having moved to the left, does not move back to the right at the start of the downswing. You see, by moving to the left, it has changed the angle of the right leg dramatically, enabling it to brace itself rigidly against the ground.

Now that the right hip joint is fully shifted to the left, the left hip joint must begin to travel back to a position where it can act as a pivot above a braced left leg later in the downswing. In fact, it moves through the same kind of arc as before, although in the opposite direction—that is, back and to the left. So while it is true that the left hip does move a little to the left as the downswing begins, the right hip remains stationary. What is actually happening here is not a turning of the hips but, rather, a mechanical exchanging of pivots.

How can the golfer put all this into practice? Some years ago I came up with some mental imagery which has proved enormously helpful to golfers I have offered it to. I must warn you that the imagery is rather crude, but it has proved so amazingly effective in getting the message across that I feel obliged to pass it on here, even at the expense of good taste. Imagine yourself addressing the ball. You are nicely set up, with your spine straight and your backside pointing down between your feet, when suddenly you feel an urge to break wind. The trouble is that someone is standing directly behind you. For the time being you forget all about the golf swing. Keeping your spine straight, you allow your head and upper body to move to the right, so that your backside is pointing over your left heel, out of harm's way. Remember, you are moving your body like this simply to break wind, so don't worry about your arms and the club. Let them go along for the ride. It is only after you have positioned yourself to break wind over your left heel that you proceed with your backswing. The sequence of movements is important: break wind first, swing later. The reason is that you cannot hope to turn fully or correctly about your right hip joint and right leg, which form the pivot, until they are in place and ready. So allow them to move into position first and turn on them afterwards.

MORE ABOUT LEVERS

The golf swing is, in essence, a movement of levers. To be precise: it is a two-lever flail action, the two levers in this case being the left arm and the shaft of the club. This ought to have been obvious to everyone since golf was first played, yet in a lifetime spent analysing virtually every theory advanced on golf, I have not once seen the golf swing described as a movement of a lever system. Until now, it seems, nobody has ever thought to begin at the beginning.

A good place to begin is the turning wheel, which, as we have seen (page 20), is a lever system. Since the wheel's rim travels many times further than its hub in the same time, it must travel many times faster. Well, the torso complies with exactly the same set of laws. It is the spine that turns the torso to produce radial acceleration. The arms are hinged to the torso, and they, in turn, create radial acceleration in the same way. It is important to recognize that the downswing turn is not a constant turning of the central hub at an even speed. As the torso turns to face the inside of the ball, it must be able to slow dramatically to allow the arms and the shaft of the club to catch up by the time impact is made with the ball. Indeed, if you study the great players in action, particularly the very long hitters, you will find that in many cases the upper part of the torso actually stops for an instant during the downswing to allow this catch-up and then starts to turn again to follow the arms and club.

This explains why golfers who try to hit with their hands encounter so many problems. Because they are trying desperately to get their hands at the ball, their arms outspeed the turning torso, which, mechanically, wreaks havoc on the golf swing. I spoke earlier of the need to eliminate slack from the system so that as much as possible of the energy generated by the turning torso can be transmitted to the clubhead. To eliminate slack, every golfer must obey a cardinal rule—never allow the arms to move faster than the torso rotates. The torso, the arms, the hands on the ends of the arms, and the shaft held by the hands—all these must move as one in a sweeping arc that is wide enough to force the arms to be fully

MORE ABOUT LEVERS

extended from the torso so that all of the joints involved become locked in position.

Acceleration of the clubhead is the product of a classic lever function—the two-lever flail action. The two-lever flail was one of mankind's earliest mechanical inventions. Flails were certainly used by

Down through the centuries peasants have threshed wheat by beating it with a flail. This was a classic two-lever action, producing tremendous acceleration at the end of the flail. The golf swing is a two-lever flail action, too, the two levers being the left arm and the club shaft.

In the first photograph of the famous golfer Curtis Strange, note how the butt is well ahead of the clubhead. In the following shot, note the distance the clubhead has moved in relation to the distance the butt has moved. The clubhead is clearly travelling at a much greater speed than the butt, which is being slowed down by the hands.

the ancient Egyptians to separate grain, and there is evidence that they may be even older than this. Typically, a flail consists of a handle (the primary lever) and a wooden bar (the secondary lever) connected by a free hinge. The obvious mechanical advantage it offers is that the top end of the bar can be made to travel at great speed by a relatively slow movement of the bottom end of the handle. So it is with the golf swing. There is a primary lever (the firmly extended left arm) which has a secondary lever (the club shaft) attached to it at a free hinge (the wrist). It is interesting to note that, in terms of mechanics, the hands holding the shaft are not part of the left-arm lever but, rather, of the shaft lever. In other words, the wrists become the free-hinge system.

All this illustrates again the absurdity of the idea that the wrists are *consciously* released just before impact. The wrists act purely as free hinges. If they didn't, the flail action could not work.

The shaft produces the flail action late in the downswing by accelerating through the angle between the left arm and the shaft. The second lever needs to catch up with the first lever by impact, at which point the left arm and the shaft are then more or less in a straight line. To catch up like this, the shaft needs to accelerate at massive speed. Here we have the answer to the question of why some players who apparently put little effort into their golf swing are able to hit further than other players who put in a lot of effort. These are the slower-moving power hitters. The law governing the case is this: maximum acceleration of a secondary lever can be achieved only if the hinge with the primary lever is stationary during the period of final acceleration. In other words, the slower the butt end is moving in the final phase of clubhead acceleration, the faster the clubhead accelerates.

If you look at action photos of the great players, like those of Curtis Strange opposite, you will see their golf swings have an interesting thing in common—the butt end of the shaft arrives at ball level far in advance of the clubhead. The hands virtually stop as the clubhead starts to catch up with them, and in an instant after impact the clubhead overtakes the hands. Thus, it may be said that the hands lead the clubhead down to impact and that the clubhead then leads the hands up.

The implications of all this are obvious. The slower and more controlled the descent of the arms-hands unit towards impact, the more easily they can be decelerated to stop in the impact zone to allow the clubhead to catch and pass them, thus achieving maximum acceleration

MORE ABOUT LEVERS

at the moment of impact. Conversely, the faster the arms at impact, the slower the clubhead. This ought to convince any golfer of the folly of swiping with the arms and slashing with the hands.

A word of warning: don't overdo it and move your arms more slowly than you have to to satisfy the other needs of the swing. This is what timing and rhythm are all about. By experimenting, find the pace of arm movement and torso rotation that is your personal ideal, then groove it in and stick to it. Remember that you are what nature made you. The reason the golfer next to you is hitting 30 metres (30 yards) further may be that his physical and mental composition, his balance factors and the physical balance of his moving parts are genetically superior to yours, and there is nothing you can do about that.

Because we are such complex mechanisms, no simple ruse or gimmick can reduce our handicap from 25 to 5 overnight, so it is pointless searching for one. The only way to improve your game is by understanding better what you are trying to do and why you are trying to do it. The reason people buy golf books and videos, take golf lessons, and switch from one golf guru to another is that they are searching for something that they cannot even identify. It may be that you were successful at other sports. You could swim, run, jump, and catch or kick a ball, yet you can't play golf for beans. Why not? The fact is that these other actions are more compatible with natural movement, so the human mechanism can perform them more easily. The problem with the golf swing is that it is not a natural movement—you must make your arms and hands do what nature did not design them to do. This, remember, is the real challenge of golf.

THE CONQUEST OF FEAR

I have already drawn attention to the fact that the majority of golfers don't really *enjoy* playing golf. Indeed, it has always seemed to me that 90 per cent of golfers never manage to extract from golf more than 10 per cent of the pleasure that the game offers. This is a very sad state of affairs, and **if this book did no more than help readers get more enjoyment from golf by reshaping their attitude to it, then I would feel it had succeeded.** Golf is a game of penalties— the trees and the water and the sand aren't put on the golf course for golfers to admire but for golfers to fear. Yet what precisely is the golfer afraid of? The trees and water and sand cannot themselves do him any harm. No, the cause of the fear is the system of penalties—the numbers game.

Humans have been rearranging the landscape for thousands of years, but in only a few instances have they succeeded in matching or improving on the beauty of nature. The golf course is often one of them. The hours you spend going around the course ought to be hours of delight and freedom from everyday cares. The golfer might well respond to this by saying, sure, he would enjoy the delights of the course a lot more if he could only hit the ball a lot better. Well, herein lies a paradox. You must first learn to hit the ball without fear of the possible consequences and, only after that, to write down the numbers. This is not to say you should adopt a bull-at-the-gate attitude. Rather, you should first weigh up all the variables; second, decide what you have to do; and, third, execute that decision without fear of what may happen.

What I have suggested here is actually the essence of positive thinking. It leaves the golfer no way out, no easy excuse path, no cushions. Either you have the courage to do what you have decided should be done or you don't have it. If you don't have it, you cannot buy it, steal it, or disguise from yourself the fact that you don't have it. Courage has to be earned the hard way. You can buy books and videos and study how the champions swing a club, but that alone can never make you a great player. If you watch, say, Jack Nicklaus in action, all

THE CONQUEST OF FEAR

you see is the external, visible dimension of his golf swing. You don't see the courage that underpins every shot he plays. Courage is the fuel that drives the human machine to greater heights. If you want to play like Nicklaus, I suggest you have a long, hard talk with your inner self before you go pounding thousands of balls a week in pursuit of the dream. Nicklaus freed himself of fear, so he was able to soar like an eagle. If fear has reduced you to a sparrow, no amount of lessons or new clubs will help you fly any higher.

Golfers often perish on the course because the hazards on the left and the right make the fairway in between seem to grow smaller and smaller. Instead of allowing the hazards to bully him into submission, the golfer must confront them. Having calmly considered the various shots he might play, he must choose one of them and then, thinking to himself, "To hell with the consequences!", play it as positively as he can.

Nobody can rid the golfer of his fear except himself, and the best place to start is at the first tee the next time he plays. If he cannot overcome it—if he is beaten into cowardly submission at each hole by having to write a number on a card—then he is in for many hours of misery, and I have no sympathy for him. If he is a slave to a silly numbers game, then he is not a golfer in the proudest traditions of the game, and, frankly, he oughtn't to be on the golf course. Such a golfer would be better off putting aside this book and reading another which tells him what he wants to hear. He will end up playing worse, but at least he won't have to confront his inner self.

Fear can affect the golfer in countless ways. I pointed out before that none of the good golfers tries to hit straight—they all either fade the ball or draw it. Discovering this, the ordinary golfer with a natural tendency to, say, fade the ball will set himself correctly to hit from left to right. He opens his stance and starts to aim for the left, but his fear of having the ball end up on the left is too great, and subconsciously he adjusts the stroke to try to hit it straight. He doesn't have the courage to start the ball left deliberately and allow the natural ball flight to bring it back to centre. Physically he is set to hit left, but mentally he is committed to the middle. The result of this cowardice is usually a dreadful cut slice.

Here is a method of overcoming this fear which you can use in partnership with a golfing friend. Having worked out what you each do most naturally—drawing or fading—the two of you should go around

THE CONQUEST OF FEAR

the course together, each trying to hit the ball in directions specified by the other. Let's say you hit naturally left to right. First, invite your partner to choose a hazard on the left. When he has done this, place a coin on the ground, close to your ball, so that it is lined up with the hazard. The challenge then will be to ignore everything else and hit the ball over the coin with your natural swing—that is, towards the hazard. Ironically, the fear of failing in the eyes of your partner will enable you to overcome your fear of starting the ball out to the left.

To play golf that satisfies you at your own level of skill, two essentials are required. One, you must have a clear understanding of what it is, mechanically, you are trying to do with your body when you swing a club, so that you can get the clubhead moving in the right direction every time with minimum fuss and maximum effect. Two, you must focus your mind on the present (that is, the control of your various moving parts during the golf swing) instead of the future (that is, how and where the ball will end up). Devote all your physical and mental energies to getting the ball started in the right direction relative to your chosen swing shape, and let the rest happen.

Years ago Gary Player observed wryly in an article that, although he could hit 800 balls a day for month after month on the practice range without hooking even once, on the first tee in a tournament that day he had hooked the ball out of bounds. Player professed to be puzzled by this, but the explanation was simple enough: there are no hazards and penalties on the practice range. Even the great players—and few have been greater or more courageous than Player—occasionally fall victim to a fleeting fear of failure. The fear is seldom in the conscious mind, where Player could have dealt with it in his own way. Usually, it is deep in the subconscious mind. In this case, the cause was probably a hazard on the right. Player's clubhead probably got outside the line, his right hand rolled the clubface to look away from the hazard, and the ball was pulled left. The real penalty Player would have paid for this was not one faulty shot but a sudden self-doubt. Despite all his success on the practice range, he could now no longer be *certain* he would play the shot he wanted to play.

In human thought, the negative is ever present. To overpower it, the positive must actively be sought out and set firmly in place. Try to identify your strongest fears and deal with them head-on. This doesn't mean attacking a shot with mindless aggression. An orderly retreat from danger is more positive than a headstrong charge to defeat. Let's say you have developed a left-to-right golf shot you can rely on, but on this occasion the hazards are on the right. Moreover, the fairway slopes a little left to right, and there is a strong breeze blowing across it from the left. To attack here could be foolhardy. Better to retreat in good order. Choose a club that carries the least risk and resign yourself to sacrificing distance. In such a positive frame of mind, there is a good chance you will hit a solid second shot on or near the green and still make par. At worst, you will escape with a rock-solid bogey and walk off feeling good about it, because you were *in control* of the situation. And remember: the breeze blowing from the left that made things difficult here will be blowing from the right on some other hole.

Golf is unique among sports in that it offers an exclusively personal challenge. There is very, very little room in golf for making excuses. In team sports you can always blame your team-mates, or the referee, or the bounce of the moving ball. In sports such as football that require physical courage it isn't so hard to work up a head of steam. But golf is played on your own and in cold blood. Golf produces a subtle and insidious fear, and it can come at you from both the past and the future. You might be playing on a course where you've always had problems on the 16th hole. Today, you're on a roll. You've played the first seven holes superbly and you're brimming with confidence. But as you walk from the 7th green, the 16th hole comes into view, stirring old, unpleasant memories. As you walk to the 8th tee, you find yourself thinking not only of the 16th but of the 13th and 18th, which have also caused you problems. Suddenly, the 8th hole seems threatening. The confidence of a few minutes before has oozed away. Your mistake was not *forcing* your mind to concentrate on the job in hand.

Here is a rule of life that has served me well over the years: if you dont like something, change it. If you meet it head-on but cannot change it, then walk away from it and forget it. If you choose to do neither of these, then learn to live with the misery that will surely come your way. Consider again the case of the golfer who has unpleasant memories of the 13th, 16th and 18th holes. He can't change the holes, so he must change his attitude to them. Instead of fearing them, he should accept them as challenges and look forward with anticipation to tackling them. You might collect a few scars by taking this positive approach, but remember that scars are always found on heroes, rarely on cowards.

WOMEN IN GOLF

In golf, being a woman is both an advantage and a disadvantage. The disadvantage is obvious. On the whole, women are smaller, lighter and not so strong as men. This isn't a problem in itself. Some of the world's greatest golfers have been quite small. The problem arises when the woman golfer goes to buy a set of clubs, because nine times out of ten the ones sold to her will be too heavy. Only a tiny percentage of women have the strength and the co-ordination to swing the clubs they usually buy for themselves. At the same time, their clubs are nearly always too short, a problem that they share with the men. So my first advice to women golfers is to use lighter and longer clubs than women are accustomed to using.

A woman golfer can do a lot to compensate for her lack of strength by taking special care to ensure that no slack is allowed to enter her swinging mechanism. In earlier chapters I described how slack can erode the power of the swing, so that only part of the force generated at the start of the downswing ends up being delivered by the clubhead to the ball. Because a woman starts the downswing with less force, she must strive to conserve as much of that force as she can, and the way to do that is by making sure her swinging mechanism is locked together and rigid.

Because they are smaller and physically weaker, women are prone to several particular faults of technique. The most glaring of these is that they try to stay behind the ball, no doubt because they feel they have to get all their weight into the shot. This error of technique is as disastrous for women as it is for men. **A woman will improve her game dramatically if she learns to finish her swing with her head over her left foot.** I suggest that women should try to position themselves so that the ball is near the middle, rather than towards the front, of the stance. That way, they are likely to find it easier to hit *down* on the ball, as they are supposed to do, instead of staying behind the ball and scooping it.

Another fault that seems particularly prevalent among women is leaving the hips behind and flicking the head to the left early in the

This series illustrates to perfection the greater flexibility of the female golfer. Because physically they are not as strong as men, women need a longer arc to generate clubhead speed.

downswing. What seems to happen here is that in an attempt to generate extra power women try to hit with their hands, and in doing so they are thrown out of balance, spin forward out of the shot, and finally fall back on their right leg. What the woman golfer must realize is that she won't generate the extra power she needs by hitting hard at the ball, but rather by following strictly the mechanical principles of the correct golf swing which I have set out in earlier chapters. By hitting hard at the ball, all she does is accelerate the butt of the club, not the head. If she swung more slowly, she would hit the ball further.

I said before that being a woman can be an advantage in golf. In fact, women golfers enjoy several advantages. In my experience, they are not so fiercely competitive on the golf course as men. They are not driven by ego to try to prove they are better than their peers, as men tend to be. As a result, they enjoy their golf more than men, and I admire them for doing so. Moreover, I have found women to be more supple than men on the whole, especially in the hips, which makes them particularly well equipped to execute a fluent swing. Their potential for improvement is unlimited.

Another demonstration of the greater flexibility of the female golfer. Observe that although the clubhead has dropped below the horizontal, she maintains a straight and firm left arm and a firm, full-fingered grip on the club.

POSTSCRIPT

If you have read this far, your views on the golf swing must by now have been transformed. Many of the things you believed about the golf swing before you opened this book have been shown to have little or no value. I was asked recently to condense in a sentence or two my entire philosophy about the golf swing. This is what I said in reply: "The golf swing is essentially a natural movement, one part of which, however, must be consciously controlled. So learn to control that one part rigidly, but surround it with the most natural sequence of movements you personally are capable of." Perhaps I have should have added: "And free your game from the shackles of symmetrics." I haven't any doubt that an obsession with symmetrics has caused golfers more problems than anything else in the game.

My final advice is: get out on the course and enjoy yourself. In the words of Walter Hagan, put the ball down, hit it, chase it, and hit it again—and while you're doing it, take the time to smell the flowers and listen to the birds. Shed all those feelings of fear that have been plaguing your game. If every bunker or pond or every golfer with a handicap fills you with fear, you shouldn't be out on a golf course. I once told a player who was beset with this kind of fear: "If you want to punish yourself, buy yourself a whip. It's a lot cheaper than a set of golf clubs." Above all, trust yourself. Strive to be as good at the game as your natural ability will allow you to be. Then, you'll be a satisfied golfer.